PRAISE FOR
CRUSH SELF-SABOTAGE & LIVE FULLY!

If you are a visual artist at any level in your career, you will want to read this valuable resource. Dr. Yanina lays out in very concise and practical terms the strategies to tackle the real hurdles we artists experience—hurdles that are products of our mindsets. The down-to-earth perspective of Sergio's experience with how he faces negative mindsets as an artist himself is powerful and illuminating.

This book is all about empowering us as artists to take action to live! As a professional artist for over thirty years, I am so relieved that I have *Crush Self-Sabotage & Live Fully!* as a treasured guide going forward!

—Christine Blair, MFA
Visual Artist

There are many wellness methods available to help with our general daily health, but none deal with the artistic temperament and well-being directly—until now. *Crush Self-Sabotage & Live Fully! The Artist's Wellness Journey to Confidence and Success* provides understanding of the artistic mindset and reveals how to carefully connect the creative synapses so that we artists are prepared emotionally and mentally before we step into our studios. This book will be the first thing you read each day and the very last thing you'll read at night.

—Drew Harris
Visual Artist

Dr. Yanina and Sergio Gomez share a heartfelt passion for supporting artists as well-rounded professionals. While they teach artists how to build a successful and financially viable business, they are just as concerned that artists thrive as individuals who enjoy a balanced life. I trust their guidance because it is based on experience and not theory. They have helped hundreds of artists achieve success on their terms. Passion, caring, and expertise—Dr. Yanina and Sergio Gomez have the qualities that make *Crush Self-Sabotage & Live Fully* a worthwhile and insightful read.

—Carrie Lannon, BA
Founder and Principal, Lannon Consulting
Former Vice President of Strategic Partnerships for Merchandise Mart Properties, Inc., The Armory Show

Crush Self-Sabotage and Live Fully is a practical, comprehensible, and effective approach to the fears and blocks artists might encounter. Collaboration with a practicing artist makes the discussion complete. This is a helpful guide for artists at any level.

—Joyce C. Morishita, PhD Art History
Professor Emeritus

Tired of the nagging voices in your head that say you are not enough—that your art isn't good enough? The power of this thoughtful and practical guide to ending self-sabotage resides in the authors' belief in artists. Born out of their own lived experiences, *Crush Self-Sabotage and Live Fully!* is written in a warm and engaging conversational style. Dr. Yanina Gomez and Sergio Gomez offer richly illustrated examples and approaches that we can turn to time and again. It shows us how to enhance our positivity and reframe our mindset to experience freedom from self-doubt and the grip of a well-intentioned inner critic gone rogue so we may flourish as the healthy creative human beings we already are.

—Jennifer Pazienza, PhD Art Education
Artist and Educator

CRUSH SELF-SABOTAGE AND LIVE FULLY!

The Artist's Wellness Journey to Confidence and Success

A. YANINA GOMEZ, PHD
AND
SERGIO GOMEZ, MFA

AUTHOR ACADEMY elite

Copyright © 2022 Adlin Yanina Gomez, PhD & Sergio Gomez, MFA
All rights reserved.

Published by Author Academy Elite
P.O. Box 43, Powell, OH 43035
www.AuthorAcademicElite.com

All rights reserved. Any unauthorized reprint or use of this material is prohibited. No part of this publication may be reproduced, stored in a retrieval system, or transmitted in any form or by any means—for example, electronic, photocopy, recording—without express prior written permission from the author.

Paperback ISBN: 979-8-88583-067-6
Ebook ISBN: 979-8-88583-068-3
Library of Congress Control Number: 2022907274

This book is dedicated to our children Alec and Nyah for being our #1 cheerleaders. We are also grateful to our outstanding global artist community, who have supported our endeavors and been our greatest inspiration to write this book. Finally, our gratitude to our God for enlightening us with the message we share in this book.

CONTENTS

FOREWORD ix
INTRODUCTION xiii

PART ONE:
OVERCOMING MY FEARS AND LIBERATING MYSELF

CHAPTER ONE: ASSESSING MY INNER SELF 3
CHAPTER TWO: IGNITING MY INNER FUEL 16
CHAPTER THREE: SCOOPING OUT MY MINDSET BLOCKS 25
CHAPTER FOUR: FREEING MYSELF FROM NEGATIVE THINKING 39

PART TWO:
LIVING FULLY AND CREATING WITH PURPOSE

CHAPTER FIVE: GETTING ORGANIZED AND MAKING THINGS HAPPEN 67
CHAPTER SIX: TRUSTING MYSELF ONCE AND FOR ALL 86
CHAPTER SEVEN: REWIRING MY MIND THROUGH PERSONAL AFFIRMATIONS 112
CHAPTER EIGHT: DETOXIFYING AND LIVING MY LIFE TO THE FULLEST 135

FINAL THOUGHTS 169
BIBLIOGRAPHY 173
APPENDIX 175
ABOUT THE AUTHORS 177

FOREWORD

If you are reading this, you have taken the first step of your journey toward success, and I must congratulate you. To quote the old Chinese proverb, "A journey of a thousand miles begins with one step." You are here because you are ready to take the next step and embark on your life's journey.

When I was a young graduate school student, my father asked me what I planned to do with a master's degree in art history. At the time, I had no idea. "What I plan to do is go to lunches and cocktail parties," I quipped.

It wasn't a lie. What I realize now is that even then, I knew my success wasn't hinged on a degree or letters after my name. My success was something that would unfold along my journey. I knew surrounding myself with like-minded art professionals would expand my mind so I would recognize opportunities I had not yet even begun to imagine.

Dr. Yanina, Sergio, and I first met while in college. Sergio and I shared studio art classes for life drawing and painting. I am the first to admit that Sergio was always a much better visual artist than I. Through Sergio, I met his wife, Dr. Yanina, who was studying psychology. Our mutual love for fine art and culture has been the foundation of our friendship and professional relationship for nearly three decades. One of our favorite things to do over the years has been ideating creative endeavors. Dr. Yanina and Sergio have been a source of inspiration and support throughout my professional life and personal life.

I eventually moved away from curatorial and museum work to dive head-first into fine art appraising and art advisory. Dr. Yanina and Sergio remained steadfast in their passion for helping artists. They expanded their outreach and developed programs to teach the art business, artistic growth, professional development, self-awareness, and wellness to artists. They have become an anchor in the art community. Over the decades, their work has touched thousands of artists worldwide. They remain a constant beacon of light and inspiration for those fortunate to know them.

Collectively, we have worked with thousands of artists at varying levels of success in a variety of ways. We discussed avenues for success artists have embarked upon, including what worked, what didn't work, and why. We spoke about what tools we believed successful artists possessed. We determined from these hours of conversation there was no single avenue to achieve success.

We agree that while each person's roadmap to success was unique, there are universal practices successful artists apply. The reason most artists fail is they stand in the way of their success. Historically speaking, no amount of gallery support, artworks sold, inclusion in significant collections, or even quality exhibitions can overcome the damage self-sabotaging behavior will do to an artist's career. Self-limiting beliefs and negative self-talk have ruined the careers of many talented promising artists before they ever really had a chance to succeed. We all have anecdotal stories of artists who peaked too young or stopped selling art after showing at MOMA or the Whitney Museum. The purpose of this book is to prevent this tragedy from recurring in contemporary art history.

Dr. Yanina and Sergio's commitment to teaching artists how to recognize self-limiting behaviors and steps for personal and professional growth is how this book came about. I applaud their ongoing dedication to addressing head-on the single largest underlying cause of professional failure. It is because of their compassion for artists and other creatives that they developed a customizable strategy for success based on individual expressions of success and self-reflection.

Success comes to those who are most adaptable to change. Adversely, our brains are hard-wired to protect us from the dangers of the unknown. Learning to process change and interpret new information is vital to our adaptability. We train our brains to seek out things foreign to us as a way to protect ourselves from a surprise attack. In extreme cases, the brain can kick into action and save lives without our being aware we are reacting. In non-life-threatening events, our brain creates thoughts about what we do not understand. Those thoughts become our beliefs. Those beliefs create behaviors. We don't even realize we do what we do most of the time. Many behaviors become toxic self-sabotage and negative self-talk without our ever being fully aware we are doing it.

What is unique about this book is how the authors dismantle how our behaviors are rooted in our thoughts. Dr. Yanina addresses ways to identify these thoughts that affect our behaviors. There is an abundance of practical and actionable steps that guide the reader toward self-transformation. The book explains how to overcome limiting beliefs, toxic thoughts, and self-destructive behaviors through self-awareness exercises. It demonstrates how mindfulness is the key to overcoming self-sabotaging thoughts and behaviors.

The essence of the book is not circumscribed to visual artists only. The mindfulness techniques and exercises apply to any endeavor marred by self-sabotaging behaviors. These tools are adaptable to any area in life needing growth and wellness. The skills learned through these exercises generate awareness of the many ways we interfere with our happiness and success. Through these exercises, we free ourselves to create a path forward.

This book is imperative for visual artists' growth because Dr. Yanina and Sergio offer step-by-step instructions on how to create a personal roadmap with self-defined achievable goals. By participating in the exercises outlined in the following chapters, the reader can build a personalized roadmap using the wisdom, tools, and techniques needed for each journey.

I urge you to take the time to learn how your unconscious beliefs limit your success and apply the practical measures to overcome them as outlined in this book. This book offers you valuable solutions to progress as an artist. Those who are open to change and hold themselves accountable for their self-sabotaging behaviors and beliefs will become masters of their destiny.

—**Ruth Crnkovich**, MA in Art History
Fine Art Advisor

INTRODUCTION

Congratulations on prioritizing and investing in your mindset and emotional wellness! Sergio and I are so happy you're accepting our challenge to believe in yourself, live fully, and create! You and I know that to live life to its fullest and create freely, we must take care of ourselves from the inside out.

As creatives, it's no surprise that self-doubt, fears, and the what-ifs can affect our creativity and taint our attempts to share it with the world. At the end of the day, our creations are a reflection of our inner world, vulnerability, personal values, ideas, and beliefs. Sometimes, the voices in our heads are so loud they dry up our inspiration and creativity. When we least expect it, our creativity stops flowing, withers, and, if we aren't careful, it can even cease to exist. Additionally, stress can overpower our thoughts. Consequently, we end up questioning ourselves and our abilities and feeling defeated.

For the past years, Sergio and I have worked alongside thousands of artists through our art career development and wellness workshops, extensive social media content, and the Art NXT Level Academy. The Academy is an online-based platform we founded where we teach artists the ins and outs of creating a successful art career and maintaining healthier emotional wellness. The more we talk with artists about the challenges and hurdles they face as creatives, the more we are convinced you must invest in your wellness to optimize your creativity and become the best version of yourself, especially your mind and emotional states.

Our mind is powerful. It houses our motivation, affection, behaviors, perception, intentions, cognitive systems, and how we reason. How we perceive ourselves and others determines how we adapt, accept or react to the world around us. Keeping a healthy state of mind is critical to living a gratifying life and coping with life's challenges. As you cultivate and nurture your mind, you will have the strength you need to conquer roadblocks that may come your way. That's why, we believe when we intentionally invest in our mindset and emotional wellness, we are improving our mental state, living a life with purpose, and setting ourselves up for greatness.

The purpose of this book is to share practical advice to help you believe in yourself, think big and positively, experience freedom, and adopt a healthier lifestyle. It will guide you as you identify, acknowledge, and overcome mindset blocks or self-sabotaging thoughts that trigger self-doubt, blocking your creativity, and prevent you from moving forward in your personal and professional journeys. In this book, you will find tools to help you create a practical strategy to conquer emotional pitfalls successfully so you can focus on growing your art career confidently.

It is important to come with an open mind, intentionality, a compassionate attitude, curiosity, and willingness to make changes in your life for the better. In this book, we'll focus on the parts of you or inner voices whose goal is to protect you from possible pain, chaos, and the unknown. These internal protectors often manifest themselves as your inner critic. We'll also tap into the parts of you that motivate you to grow and become your best self.

Before we keep going, let's take a moment to define mindset blocks. Mindset blocks are thoughts and feelings sabotaging or preventing us from challenging ourselves and taking initial steps that lead to personal growth and reaching our potential. What-ifs, fear, and insecurities are examples of mindset blocks.

- What if I'm not a good enough artist?
- What if no one wants to buy my work?
- What if I lose my gallery representation?
- What if I ditch my nine-to-five job to become a full-time artist and fail?

We all experience mindset blocks repeatedly. The good news is mindset blocks are a sign you're heading in the right direction! The more aspirations and goals you set for yourself, and the more you challenge yourself to grow, the more likely it is you will experience mindset blocks. See, you're not alone! If you don't address these feelings, however, hoping they will go away one day, you might end up facing defeat. But that is not you. You decided to purchase this book. You're determined to make things happen for yourself. Now you know there's nothing wrong with you experiencing mindset blocks, let's keep going.

As you challenge yourself beyond your comfort zone, don't be surprised when your mind chooses to default on fears and doubts to keep you within the comfort zone and feeling safe. Your mind craves comfort and things that are easy to process. When you begin to explore possibilities beyond what's familiar, your internal protectors will likely react. Often, it is manifested as self-doubt or self-sabotaging behaviors that hold you back.

In each chapter, I'll be sharing practical advice and what you can do to help you identify and overcome your mindset blocks (over and over again), live a healthier lifestyle, believe in yourself, and feel confident about sharing your art with the world. Each chapter also includes a section titled *Sergio's Take*. In this section, you'll receive Sergio's point of view and response, along with practical recommendations to help you apply what you learn into your personal and career journeys, including the topics of organization, exposure, marketing, and sales.

Through the self-guided inner reflection exercises found under the *Diving Deeper* section, you'll be able to go within and focus on inner work. You'll identify and clear mindset blocks preventing you from trusting yourself and reclaiming your creative confidence. You'll also be going through steps designed to help you address toxic relationships and replace unhealthy habits with new, healthy patterns that lead to living life to its fullest.

Change won't happen unless you take the time to do the necessary inner and outer work. That's why we encourage you to commit to doing the work and be intentional about your journey. We invite you to schedule time, once a week, to read a chapter and complete the *Diving Deeper* section of each chapter. This is going to be your "me time." As much as you can, make sure you find a space where you won't be distracted or interrupted. Call it your special place for curiosity and introspection. You can keep your area quiet, use a noise machine, play soothing background music, or blast off your heavy metal rock playlist if that helps you concentrate! Light a few candles or open up the windows and feel the fresh breeze coming in. Do whatever works best for you.

If you're somewhat like us, make sure you add your "me time" to your schedule and set a reminder on your phone. Turn off your phone during your "me time." If you need to keep it on, make sure you turn off your alerts. They can be very distracting. You can ask Sergio about this! There was a time his phone alerts were chiming so often it felt like we were in the middle of a cricket invasion. Sigh!

We encourage you to partner up with an artist friend or colleague. Invite them to support you or go through this book together. Become each other's accountability partner. Another idea to help you stay focused on completing this journey is printing a reminder and setting it in your studio. It can read as, *work on my wellness journey on Fridays.* Or perhaps *work on my "Believe in Yourself, Live Fully, and Create journey"* will work better for you. Finally, take action and document your progress in the designated areas of the book. You can also use a wellness journal. Document your wins, and focus on your personal gains and the progress you're making. Celebrate each success, even if it seems small. Any victory is worth celebrating!

Keep in mind mindset blocks come and go. Today, you may be feeling very confident and ready to conquer the world. Tomorrow, something may trigger self-doubt, and your inner critic will get back on business. The strategies you'll learn in this book will help you address and overcome current and future self-sabotaging thoughts. That's why we suggest you keep it handy. Remember, change won't happen unless you make it happen! Use this book as your journal to document your journey!

You can experience success and greater satisfaction and release your unlimited creativity. It's your time to shine, believe in yourself once and for all, and live fully. Sergio and I can't wait to see your growth as you take the time to dive in, embrace, and explore your inner world to make the necessary changes in your life to create and live fully!

PART ONE
OVERCOMING MY FEARS AND LIBERATING MYSELF

CHAPTER ONE
ASSESSING MY INNER SELF

It's Monday morning. The sun is shining, the birds are chirping, and the weather is perfect. It's the start of what you expect to be an amazing week. You're kicking off the day with your favorite wake-me-up drink, grab your phone, open up your inbox, and there it is. You received an email from a well-respected curator announcing a call for artists at a prestigious gallery. Your first reaction was filled with excitement and hope. Already, you're imagining your art in the show and chatting with possible buyers during the opening night, telling them all about your inspiration and process.

You're so thrilled about the possibility and decide to click on the link provided in the email. As you reach out to click on the link, you immediately stop yourself. Right away, you begin to hear the voice of your inner protector telling you this opportunity is way above your head. It means you're not ready for a chance like this and discourages you from trying because you're going to be disappointed again. Next, your inner critic chimes in and tells you that your art is not good enough and you're not good enough.

Suddenly, the tingling in your belly, the excitement running all over your body, and the picture you painted in your head about the opening night abruptly disappeared. You begin to justify to yourself why you shouldn't even click on the link. You begin to tell yourself maybe your art is not ready for this show. You also tell yourself you don't want to experience another disappointment. Granted, you haven't even clicked on the link that takes you to the details of the call for artists. You tell yourself you're not spending money on the submission fee because finances are tight. You hear loud and clear, *this opportunity is not for artists like you.* The morning that started so well suddenly ended up triggering your insecurities and messing up the rest of your day.

Do you relate to this story? Have you experienced something like this before? Perhaps, you wanted to introduce yourself to a gallery owner or curator but found yourself thinking of all possible excuses to avoid taking that step. Or maybe, you finished your amazing body of work and feel stuck and unsure about what to do next. You're not into social media marketing or sales. Let alone trying to convince a gallery owner to represent you. If this is you, my dear artist, you may be experiencing mindset blocks. When we are not as confident when fears and insecurities invade our heads when we're constantly questioning ourselves and our abilities, we're experiencing mindset blocks.

As I've mentioned in the Introduction, experiencing mindset blocks can signify you're heading in the right direction. This intense activity happening in your head may have been triggered by your desire to experience success in your art career! But, you have to be careful and know when to acknowledge your inner protector and move forward! The more space you give your inner critic to rehearse these mindset blocks in your head, the more likely you'll feel intimidated, insecure, or possibly paralyzed. Consequently, mindset blocks can potentially lead you to frustration and giving up.

In my experience, I've found we're our worst enemy. We are harsh and judgmental toward ourselves, so we end up experiencing mindset blocks and self-sabotage. When you suppress or ignore these thoughts hoping they'll disappear, you'll likely miss your opportunity to move your art career to the next level.

In the past, we've worked with highly talented artists who put too much emphasis on what if's (what if no one likes my artwork?), fears (I won't submit my work to this specific show because I'll be rejected), false assumptions (I don't have an MFA, and therefore, I won't be taken seriously), or technology barriers (I can't learn new apps at my age).

Let's think about that for a second. When your mindset blocks are not addressed, and you're too busy worrying about them, your mind and body consume a lot of energy to deal with these emotions, and not much is left to use when you need it. Consequently, we stop trying.

If you want to overcome your mindset blocks, you have to be intentional about it. You've got to commit to changing how you see and interpret situations. It's time for a mindset and perspective upgrade! Are you ready to conquer the mindset blocks preventing you from moving forward in your journey and creative path? I hear a yes! Let's focus on what matters: growing as a person and managing your art career confidently.

The first step is to check in and pay attention to what's happening inside of you. Take the time to assess your inner self. Are you hearing your inner critic loudly or perhaps a soft voice encouraging you to pursue opportunities and try new things? What toxic thoughts are emerging often that, perhaps, are rooted in your past? What makes you who you are? Is your inner critic loud and boisterous? If so, I encourage you to acknowledge and listen to it. Don't try to ignore or suppress it. Have you tried to ignore a toddler in a grocery store who's throwing the worse tantrum because he wants a piece of candy? If you have, then you know how they can get louder and louder until you either give in and purchase the candy or go through the embarrassment and put up with the dirty looks of those around you as you're running outside of the building.

The same concept applies to your internal protectors. If you ignore them, they'll get louder to get your attention. I would recommend you acknowledge your internal protectors. Remember, they are there to help you avoid a possible failure, pain, or disappointment. Although they may not show their intention compassionately, they're not your enemy. They have a role in your inner world: to avoid a system overload and feeling overwhelmed. Thank your protectors and remind them you're working on it and what matters is your growth and success, which won't happen unless you try.

Often, your inner critic can take the central role in your inner world. It's there to push your limits in a harsh and unkind manner. If you're not careful, your inner critic can crush your soul and dissolve your intentions. You can avoid letting your inner critic define who you are. As we go through this book, you'll learn strategies to calm your internal protectors, especially your inner critic, so they don't feel the need to create chaos within you.

Having a clear picture of who you are, what triggers your insecurities, and what you want to accomplish is a great start. In this chapter, we'll be diving deeper into your inner self to identify your strengths, weaknesses, insecurities, and doubts. You'll also have the opportunity to acknowledge where you are in your journey so you can reconnect with your goals and aspirations and take ownership of your today and tomorrow.

Since we already know mindset blocks can show up without warning, let's do something about it. As I've mentioned, to clear these blocks, you have to take some time to assess your inner self. I'm going to share a few reflective questions to help you get started with your inner self-assessment. But before we get to them, I invite you to begin creating a picture of who you are and what you want to accomplish.

Let's begin this process by reflecting on a few questions. If you push yourself through these questions, you might miss a few important details and powerful revelations. You don't need to write full sentences yet. I simply want to warm up your brain and help you get in the zone. You can, however, use sticky notes to jot down keywords or phrases that pop up in your head so you have them handy later. You can also use a notes app if you're more comfortable with your phone or another electronic device. Take your time!

The first question is: Who am I? I'll be the first one to admit this is a very difficult and deep question. Take a moment to think about who you are, what makes you unique, what makes you who you are. Think about what your values and beliefs are. At the end of this chapter, you'll have an opportunity to write your answers down as detailed as you want. For now, please start thinking about it and jotting down some ideas that come up as you meditate on this.

Once you have a clear picture of who you are, you must describe where you are at this moment. Where am I at this moment as a person, as an artist? Do you consider yourself an emerging artist and feel unsure about how the art world works? Maybe, you finished a new body of work and feel stuck because you don't know how to market it? Or you're an established artist selling well, but you are not sure what's next for your art career. Conversely, you may be returning to art-making after a career change and unsure how to start. Whether you are content with where you are at this moment, fulfilled or in a bad place, go ahead and name it.

Be careful with the feeling of contentment. It's great to feel content. Yet, if you aren't careful, contentment can prevent you from experiencing the growing pains that lead to becoming stronger and greater. Remember, the art world is constantly evolving and moving forward quickly. If you choose to stay content and stagnant where you are, you'll end up missing the bus.

Once you identify who you are and name where you are at this moment, it is time to define your main goal or identify a shift for yourself, your career, or both. Keep using those sticky notes! I encourage you to manifest your future right now. Lingering in a place where negativity and discontent are the norms will not help you get out of this hole. You must acknowledge your situation, make decisions, and take action.

Now, let's jump into the future for a moment. Think about where you want your artistic career to be. Neither be shy nor undersell yourself here. The sky is the limit! When you talk about your future, it doesn't have to mean ten years from now. It can be as close as two or three months from now. Don't let time discourage or slow you down. Where do you see yourself two months or two years from now? What about five or ten years from now? Perhaps, you've been creating for a while, and you feel it's time to take your art from the studio to the world. Maybe you want your creative career to be acknowledged by colleagues and experts or receive an invitation for a solo exhibition at a distinguished museum. Once again, as you allow yourself to imagine, dream, and make decisions, don't rush it. Take a moment to think about that. Remember, you'll have an opportunity to write down your answers at the end of this chapter, and those sticky notes will come in handy.

Finally, take ownership of your today and tomorrow. Yes, some circumstances out of your control can be slowing your art career down right now. You're waiting on a curator to let you know if your submission was accepted. You've been sending emails to a few local gallery owners asking for a meeting, but you haven't heard from them. Perhaps, you have a new body of work and feel clueless about how to market or sell it. The list of unfortunate events can be endless.

The truth is, you can either continue waiting on others, let yourself drown in unfortunate events, and do nothing else. Alternatively, you can focus on what you can control and keep taking action while you're waiting on others. Maybe you can write an exhibition proposal for a local art organization or university gallery while you wait on the results of that call for artists you submitted to a few weeks back. Or sign up for a social media marketing course for artists and learn how to sell your art online. Don't waste your time and energy waiting on others. Focus on what you can control and use time and energy to your advantage.

As you take ownership and responsibility for what you can control, you empower yourself while nurturing your mindset. Think about this for a second. Focus on what needs to be done to improve, grow and experience success. In other words, what do you need to do to get from point A to point B smartly?

Sergio and I have worked with artists who have strong credentials such as an MFA, produce outstanding art, and have chosen to adopt an optimistic mindset that is taking their art career to unimaginable levels. We have also worked with self-taught artists who may not appear to have all the ideal credentials and lack powerful connections or gallery representation. Yet, there's an area they are ahead of the game. They believe in abundance, their art, and trust themselves. They have invested in a healthier mindset and self-confidence that allows them to look for and consequently find great opportunities. They believe people out there who connect with their art, and they're determined to find them. There are also those artists who may appear to have all the credentials yet struggle along the way. My dear artist, it's about your mindset and taking action!

By now, you should have a rough idea of who you are, where you are at this moment, and where you want to be. You probably have a few sticky notes all over your studio or, maybe, they're covering the wall by your desk. You're ready to complete the exercises in the *Diving Deeper* section of this chapter. Again, take your time! Once you work on your inner assessment, you'll have a clearer picture of your qualities, the reality you're facing, and your ideal future. But, before you hit the *Diving Deeper* section, check out Sergio's response and advice on this topic in the *Sergio's Take* section below.

Sergio's Take

During one of our online webinars, I once met an artist who said she's never experienced mindset blocks. Wow! Wonder Woman had entered the room. I wish I were in her shoes. Perhaps, denial is the biggest mindset block. It prevents us from learning and growing. As Dr. Yanina has very eloquently explained thus far, the reality is we all experience mindset blocks and limiting beliefs. We all hear the voices of disbelief once in a while. I hear them all the time. Let me tell you how I deal with them.

The number one question I get from artists who meet me for the very first time is, "Sergio, how do you manage to be an artist, curator, gallery owner, educator, marketing expert, and having a family?" They ask as if that is some sort of superpower. It appears from a distance I have everything together and under control. The reality is, while I have become super organized and a careful curator of my time and daily activities, I experience daily mindset blocks.

Here are some voices going on right now in my head. What if nobody listens to my latest podcast? What if people don't like the Breakfast with Sergio video I recently posted? What if the show I'm curating is not well received? What if it gets a bad review? What if the artwork we picked for the next gallery promotion doesn't bring new collectors? What if we don't make enough art sales this month? What if my new art series is not as good as the previous one? What if I'm doing too much marketing? What if my contribution to this book is not as good as Dr. Yanina's? After all, she is a perfectionist and I'm a go, go, go, leave the details for later, kind of guy.

Should I go on? Do you have time to listen to the voices in my head? You get the point.

The more responsibilities you take on, the more your internal protectors and inner critics will have ammunition to shoot at you. How do I manage the loud voices of disbelief inside my head? After doing the self-assessment exercises Dr. Yanina recommends in this book, I believe I have become very good at focusing on what I can control and nothing else. I tell myself every day that this is my superpower and I must use it. If I cannot control something, I rule it out and try not to worry about it. Perhaps that is why I don't worry too much about the future, unlike my wife. I love visualizing a positive and ideal future, but I can only control what I do today to arrive at that ideal future.

I clearly remember the year 2004 when I wanted to open an art gallery in Chicago. My internal protectors kept reminding me, *Sergio, you do not have a clue about business. You do not know anything about running a gallery. You are an immigrant and at a disadvantage. You have no start-up money or savings. You do not know any collectors.*

The voices were loud and were correct in their assessment, but there was only one thing I could do. I took action on what I had control over at that moment. The only thing I had access to was people. I called friends and started knocking on doors and asking people for advice. Some never replied, but some did. I quickly learned I had to work with people if this project was to take shape. That was the only thing I could control. I asked for help and advice. Seventeen years later, 33 Contemporary Gallery is a thriving gallery.

Action is the differentiator in every scenario. Dr. Yanina has been clear in her Introduction. Without taking action, nothing happens. Take ownership of what you have control of and act upon it. When a door closes down in your face, go and knock on the next door. You may be one knock away from finding the opportunity that will change everything in your art career. What door do you need to knock on today? And, if no door opens for you, do what you love to do. I take a marker and draw my door on the wall. In other words, I create my opportunities when no one seems to believe in me.

There's more on this topic in future chapters. For now, go ahead and do your self-assessment. Become self-aware of your present reality and commit to continuing on this self-empowering journey with Dr. Yanina and me. See you in the next chapter, my friend.

Diving Deeper

Step 1: Assessing My Inner Self.

To clear our mindset blocks, we have to take some time to assess our inner self. We have to have a clear picture of who we are and what we want to accomplish. Let's begin!

- Who am I (*e.g.*, uniqueness, beliefs, values, etc.)?

_____

_____

- What has my inner critic been telling me about myself?

  _____

  _____

- What has my inner protector told me about challenging myself and moving forward? Are there any toxic thoughts often emerging that, perhaps, are rooted in my past?

  _____

  _____

- What situations, circumstances, words, phrases, or people trigger my insecurities (self-awareness)?

  _____

  _____

Now, let's identify your present.

- Where am I at this moment in my life?

  _____

  _____

Once you define who you are and where you are at this moment, it's time to express your main goal for yourself or your art business. Manifest your future.

1. I want to be/I see myself

   _____

   _____

2. I want my art business to be

   _____

   _____

3. Now that I have identified what triggers my insecurities, this is what I can do to avoid them:

   _____

   _____

Finally, take ownership of your today and tomorrow. As you do this, you're empowering yourself while nurturing your mindset.

1. What circumstances are beyond my control that I need to put aside or release?

   _____

   _____

2. What circumstances are under my control that I can use as leverage?

   _____

   _____

3. What do I need to do to ensure my choices are aligned with my priority/goal?

   _____

   _____

4. Do I have to make changes, tweak some things, or adapt to something new? Name it below.

   _____

   _____

Wrapping It Up

Congratulations on completing the Assessing My Inner Self reflection exercises. By now, you should have a clear picture of *who* you are, *where* you are at this moment, and *where* you want to be or *what* you want to accomplish (*e.g.*, personal and professional plans). Additionally, you have created a strategic plan to face your insecurities in a healthier way. In the next chapter, you'll be identifying what motivates you and defining your inner fuel.

CHAPTER TWO
IGNITING MY INNER FUEL

As I was writing this book, a new member of the Art NXT Level Academy stopped by our gallery to view the group exhibition we were featuring. As soon as he entered the gallery, I immediately noticed a lack of spark in his demeanor, though he seemed excited about coming to the gallery. After he finished viewing the show, he stopped by the desk where Sergio and I were working. He began sharing about his art career and was not shy about letting us know his frustrations and disappointments with his art career.

The first thing he said to us was, "You guys are my last hope! That's why I joined the Art NXT Level Academy."

"What do you mean?" we replied.

He said he was not even sure if he should continue pursuing his art career. "What's the point?" He said he was very frustrated because he's terrible at social media and is not selling much. He shared that he was discouraged because he doesn't understand the art market, and his art isn't selling well. "I wonder if my art truly matters."

It was crystal clear our artist friend was starting to believe his inner critic and was adopting these negative thoughts as his reality. One thing was evident that beautiful sunny afternoon; our artist friend was running out of motivation and hope.

The first thought populating my mind was, *our friend needs an intervention!* He was on the cusp of running out of his inner fuel. He was in great need of rekindling with his inner fuel to help him move forward in the face of frustration and disappointment. At that moment, I asked him the first of the few mind-blowing questions I'll be sharing with you in this chapter. "Why did you decide to become an artist?"

After a brief pause, the magic began to happen. He shared all the many reasons why he chose the art career. As he spoke, his demeanor began to change. His astonishing hazel eyes began to spark like the stars in the sky. I asked him a few other deep questions that helped him conclude his art does matter. Don't worry. At the end of this chapter, you'll be answering the same questions.

My dear artist, have you ever felt like our artist friend before? Are you feeling right now that your art or art career doesn't matter? Maybe you're questioning why you ended up choosing an art career instead of pursuing _____ (fill in the blank). Perhaps you're wondering if it's worth going through the motions of the complicated art world. In this chapter, I want to guide you to identify what motivates you to pursue your personal and professional journey. At the end of the chapter, you'll have a list of reasons or circumstances you can use as your inner fuel to ignite your motivation when the going gets tough.

Are you ready to begin exploring and identifying your inner fuel? Fantastic! I appreciate that you are ready to take action. Let's start by acknowledging the reasons why we should take the time to identify or rekindle our spark. As the unique individual you are, some things awaken your curiosity and impart purpose or meaning in your life. Some things get you excited and nurture your passions. Your fuel or spark leads you to add something marvelous to the world in your unique way. It also gives you strength and grit when life throws at you unexpected hurdles and challenges.

Now, let's focus on everything motivating you to pursue your journey, whether it's about your individual or professional growth. Now is when those sticky notes or a writing app can come in handy again. To help you with this exercise, I'll ask you a few questions. Keep in mind you'll have time and space to ponder n these questions in the *Diving Deeper* area at the end of this chapter. For now, I intend to get your thoughts rolling.

By now, you should have a clear idea of who you are, where you are at this moment, and where you want to be or what you want to accomplish (e.g., personal or professional plans). If you need a reminder, head over to Chapter One where you did an amazing work identifying and defining these areas. Now, it's time to get busy again. Let's dive into your inner fuel or inner boost!

We all have reasons behind our choices and decisions. Think about the reasons for choosing the plans or goals you identified in Chapter One. What is motivating you to complete this plan or achieve this goal? I invite you to identify the personal values and principles aligned with your plans or goals. Making plans and setting achievable goals takes an enormous amount of time, energy, and commitment. As much as you may feel like you're moving through your life and your career with direction, understand it's common to face hurdles and obstacles along the way. It's called life! That's why it's important you take stock of your values, principles, and what truly matters to you.

Think about the things that make you excited and fired up. There's little motivation for growth if your goals or plans are not connected to your values and principles. While plans and goals may change based on life circumstances, your values are often consistent. They connect us to a greater purpose in life and bring us back to our foundation and anchor.

As you take the time to list your values, principles, and what's important in your life, you will stock up yourself with the inner fuel you need to maintain the fire lit within you. This fuel comes in handy when unexpected obstacles block your path, you feel frustrated and overwhelmed, or you begin questioning your decisions. I cannot guarantee you will never run out of inner fuel. It happens! We live in a fast-paced society that takes away so much from us. It demands our constant attention, time, and energy and expects us to deliver fast results. Consequently, we find ourselves experiencing high levels of stress, anxiety, physical burnout, emotional pitfalls, and practicing harmful habits. That is when we begin to doubt ourselves, our ability, purpose, and creativity.

Keep in mind the greatest enemies of your spark are procrastination and fear. When you're experiencing self-doubt or your inner critic is bombarding you with possible reasons to stay within your comfort zone, don't try to ignore or suppress it. As you learned in Chapter One, this approach is not effective. A practical way to face this situation is coming back to the answers you give to the questions in this chapter. Simply put, remind yourself of your why.

Your *why* truly matters. Once you have a strong clarity around your true purpose or purposes, and your actions focus on supporting your why, you'll begin to shift your mindset toward a more optimistic way of thinking. You'll experience

Use your why to refuel your mind and soul.

greater satisfaction. More importantly, when you define your why, you'll have clarity and figure out the how. It's like a ripple effect. Use your why to refuel your mind and soul. Remind yourself of your why as often as you need.

I know you are ready to name your inner fuel and dive deeper into this chapter's self-guided exercises. It's also important you find out how to make room in your present situation to ignite your inner fuel. Before you do, head over *Sergio's Take* as he will be sharing with you how experiencing clarity about his why and diving into his inner fuel is making a powerful impact in his art career.

Sergio's Take

I once heard motivational speaker Tony Robbins talk about the idea that you have to believe there is a treasure out there every day, and you need to do everything in your power to go out to find it. The moment you stop believing there is a treasure is the point at which you stop trying.

When I heard this concept, I asked myself, *what is the treasure artists seek? What do we want?* To answer this question, I went back to our data. A few years back, the Art NXT Level Academy surveyed hundreds of artists worldwide at all levels of their art career, from emerging to established. We asked around 300 artists to identify the four top things they wanted most for their art careers.

After all the answers came back, we analyzed them and discovered four main categories. Here is what we found in the order of importance based on the responses to the survey.

Generally speaking, artists want:

- Freedom to create.
- Sustainable income from our work.
- Acceptance and respect from our peers.
- Opportunities to gain exposure for our art.

Do any of these resonate with you? I align with each of them as well. When I looked at the data, I realized the number one answer relates to what happens inside the studio. In contrast, the other three relate to the external factors outside our art studios, such as sales, exposure, marketing, and networking.

Let's approach the first one: freedom to create. When good things are happening inside the studio, we feel good, the sun shines brighter, the energy levels are high, and we completely lose a sense of time. We feel the flow of creativity running through every bone in our bodies. You know exactly what I mean. You have been there, and so have I. What happens when things are not working out? What happens when every painting, drawing, or whatever you create seems flat, dry, or lifeless? You begin to hear the voices Dr. Yanina speaks about in this chapter. Frustration sets in. You start resenting walking into the studio. I don't know about you, but I have been there many times—perhaps more than I would like to admit in this book.

This is one of the worst places to be in because, deep inside, you know the only one who can take you out of this dark place is you. Nobody is going to come out to create the art for you. It's all 100% on you. In those times of creative dryness, igniting your inner fuel is so important to reignite your creativity spark.

The same is true for the other three items in the list—income, acceptance, and opportunities. When opportunities are landing in your lap, everyone seems to love your work, and sales are coming in, you feel successful and empowered. Hey, who does not like to get a check in the mail or electronic funds transfer for a work you sold? Art is not about money, but you nevertheless need money to create the art that is not about money.

I recently spoke to a successfully established artist friend who was going through a dry spell in his art business. The work in the studio was going amazing, but outside the studio, things seemed to be collapsing. Shows were canceled due to the global pandemic, he experienced gallery rejections, a failed commission, and sales down to alarming numbers.

The truth is that at some point in your art career, you will face dry spells of creativity inside your studio or in your art business. Unfortunately, it may happen to be both at the same time. If that is you right now, I feel you, my friend. I have been there myself. Whether you are in this place now or not, answering the big "why" questions below in the *Diving Deeper* section of this chapter will help you get through. They will help you reignite your inner fuel. They will help you reconnect the motives behind what you do. They will remind you what it feels like to experience freedom as an artist.

You will also start to see with clarity as you remove the fog of ambiguity and distractions by answering these questions. You need clarity to make good decisions in your studio and your art business, but it only comes when we take the time to invest in ourselves and get to work. It is your turn, my friend. Commit to doing the necessary work to make it through. I leave you with this quote by one of the most notorious artists of the twentieth century.

> "Every idea occurs while you are working.
> If you are sitting around waiting for inspiration,
> you could sit there forever."
> —Chuck Close

Diving Deeper

In this section, I encourage you to think about everything that motivates you to pursue your next step, whether going back to school, writing a proposal for a solo show, or ditching your nine-to-five job to start your entrepreneurial journey.

- Why did I choose art as my career?
  _____
  _____

- What inspires or motivates me to create art?
  _____
  _____

- Why did I make this plan or select this goal(s)?
  _____
  _____

- What motivates me or who's inspiring me to accomplish this plan or goal?
  _____
  _____

- What values and principles are aligned with my plans or goals?
  _____
  _____

- At the end of the day, what matters to me is _____
  _____.

Wrapping it up

Now that you've done the hard work of inner exploration, you have at your disposal the inner fuel you'll need to get you going when life feels overwhelming. Each time you feel frustrated or doubt yourself, come back to these answers.

Remind yourself about your Why's
Use them to refuel your mind and soul.
Fan your spark!

We're ready to move on to our next step, identifying and clearing out any mindset blocks. See you in Chapter Three!

CHAPTER THREE
SCOOPING OUT MY MINDSET BLOCKS

I'm so glad you're back and ready to continue your inner journey. I know you're ready for more, but let's pause for a second to acknowledge the work you've done so far. By now, you have taken the time to assess your inner self and have a clear picture of who you are and what you want to accomplish. You took the time to dive deeper into your inner world, successfully identified your strengths, weaknesses, and insecurities, and acknowledged where you are in your journey. Maybe you've decided to rekindle and move ahead with your goals. Or you've decided to develop a plan to take ownership of your today and tomorrow. Regardless of the path you've chosen to take, I'm here to support you. You'll make it happen!

That is not all, my dear reader! You've also identified what motivates you to pursue your personal and professional journey. You created a list of reasons or circumstances you will now use as your inner fuel to ignite your motivation and spark your determination, especially when the going gets tough. Wow! You're amazing.

Let's take a moment to check in. Take a deep breath. Inhale. 1, 2, 3. Exhale. Let's take four more deep breaths. How do you feel about the progress you have made so far? I invite you to write your thoughts down on your wellness journal or somewhere around this page. I hope you're feeling proud of what you've already accomplished and excited about continuing your journey toward living your best life. You know we still have work to do, but it's very important you acknowledge and celebrate your wins, even if you label them as small. In this chapter, you will learn strategies to identify the mindset blocks that are distracting and preventing you from reaching out to your true potential. Are you ready? I can hear you saying, "Yes!" Let's get busy.

Before we go on, I want to remind you briefly why you're experiencing mindset blocks or self-sabotaging thoughts. In simple terms, it's because you're a human being who wants more out of life! You have aspirations, goals, and plans. You are not satisfied with where you are in your creative journey at this moment. You've decided to push yourself and ditch your comfort zone. You desire more for your life, but you might not be sure about where to start or how to get there. You're stepping into the unknown and choosing to be courageous.

Naturally, your internal protectors are feeling unease with your decision. Your protectors do not like your wild moves, and they're going to do whatever it takes to bring you back to what's familiar—a place where you feel safe and everything is predictable. That's when you begin to feel a high dose of self-sabotaging thoughts spreading all over your head, and you start feeling overwhelmed. That is your inner protector's way to keep you in check.

As you go through this chapter, you're going to name the what-ifs, fears, doubts, and insecurities going through your head at this moment. At the end of the chapter, you'll be able to write them down as you do your inner work. In the meantime, get those sticky notes or app handy to jot down your thoughts as needed.

Story alert! It was a gloomy, cold, and windy winter afternoon. Sergio, the kids, and I were stuck at home because a snowstorm had reached our area. By mid-morning, about five to six feet of snow had already accumulated. We were not going anywhere for a while. I received a phone call from a close artist friend. She called me to tell me a renowned international art gallery had reached out to her. They asked for her digital art portfolio because they were considering exhibiting her work at one of the international art fairs during Art Basel in Miami, FL. As you can imagine, my friend was ecstatic and very excited. She told me all about the email conversation between her and the gallery manager. Suddenly, there was silence, dead silence.

"Are you okay?" I asked. That awkward silence was taking over the conversation. "What's the matter? Aren't you excited about this opportunity?

"Yes, I am excited. I'm thrilled! As I'm sharing this with you, I realize this is going to be another disappointment in my life. I don't have the experience other artists have, and they'll probably call it off once they find out." – she said.

"Why are you saying that? This is amazing, and you deserve this opportunity," I responded.

To my surprise, her mental state completely transformed from being fired up to experiencing self-sabotage and feeling defeated before she even gave it a try. She added, "I know once my work is compared to other established artists, they'll go for their work and reject mine (she's already making excuses to avoid a possible disappointment). You know my art isn't there yet. I need to get my act together before I pursue an opportunity like this one. I know I'm not going to make it (she's self-sabotaging her skills and the opportunity). What if I go through the motions and end up being rejected? What if my art isn't good enough for this exhibition (a few more mindset blocks)?"

My dear reader, have you been in my friend's shoes before? Have you experienced self-sabotaging thoughts, like, I don't have what it takes to succeed in the art world? I don't have credentials. I don't have a lot of experience since I just started my career or returned after years in a nine-to-five job. This is not going to work for me. Maybe you're thinking, I'm not lucky enough. The competition is way better than me. It's not even worth a try. If I could only be more like so and so. But you don't stop there. You've probably asked yourself, what if I mess up, or worse, what if I fail?

Are similar thoughts distracting you from being productive and preventing you from maximizing your potential? If I guessed, I would say this is hitting home. You're probably freaking out right now, wondering how in the world I can read your mind. The truth is, I can't read your mind. Those thoughts happen more than you think. Most people who challenge themselves and think outside the box experience mindset blocks and self-sabotage. You are not alone! Once you take the first step toward greatness and innovation, you're stepping into foreign territory. You start making decisions and doing things you've never done before. Naturally, your inner thoughts, or as I call them, internal protectors, will do whatever it takes to protect you from experiencing a possible pain, failure, or disappointment.

It is time to clear your mindset blocks to regain the confidence you need to continue your personal and professional journey. If you stop now and choose to ignore or suppress your blocks, you will be holding yourself back from experiencing the results you want to see in your personal growth and creative career. Your mind will be way too busy worrying and questioning yourself about every decision you make, and you will also regret you've deprived yourself of growth. That's not you, my dear reader. I have a hunch you simply need a little push, encouragement, and some motivation. You are a go-getter and will finish this journey even if it takes a bit longer than you'd expected. I know you will no longer let these blocks stop you from defining who you are and redefining your present and future. You're ready for more!

> You are a go-getter and will finish this journey even if it takes a bit longer than you'd expected.

Let's take a moment to acknowledge your mindset blocks. We are going to start by reflecting on a few questions. Although you'll be doing deep inner work in the *Diving Deeper* section of this chapter, I would like to help you get this process started. Think about the biggest mindset block or loudest self-sabotaging thought that's been troubling you lately. I'm talking about the nagging thought that screams at you when everything is quiet around you. It's probably screaming at you right now. Could it be you feel like you're a lousy artist and incapable of succeeding in the art world? Jot it down anywhere around this page or on your sticky notes if you have them handy. What is holding you back from achieving your goals or plans? Could it be you're paying too much attention to this thought? Perhaps you have come to believe the voice that tells you're incapable of becoming a successful artist.

How far back can you go to pinpoint the root of this belief or wound? Maybe your fifth-grade teacher told you that you wouldn't make it in life because you're easily distracted and you internalized his words. What circumstances are fueling this block or thought?

Could it be you're comparing your life with that of other artists? You've been listening to the voice in your head constantly discouraging you from sharing your creativity so you save yourself from getting hateful comments on social media. Or maybe you applied to an art exhibition a few years ago, and your artwork was not selected. You felt rejected and believed the voice that kept on telling you your art wasn't good enough. Consequently, you stopped trying.

Honestly, mindset blocks are exhausting. The longer we carry them, the heavier they get. It doesn't have to be that way. It's your choice! Let's take a moment to pinpoint the root of the block or self-sabotaging thought you've identified. What circumstances are feeding this block to the point it's about to burst? I encourage you to pause your reading and give yourself some space for introspection. The work you do in this chapter is very important. Please take your time and avoid rushing through it. It might take you an hour, a few hours, or even a few days. It's okay. Permit yourself to work on this area.

Once you have identified the blocks and the roots, you will create a strategy to prove these blocks wrong. Even if you're unable to pinpoint the origin of your block or thoughts, please keep ongoing. Don't let that stop you from continuing your healing journey. In a court of law, you are innocent until proven guilty. This same tactic applies to your mindset blocks. They might seem innocent and true until proven guilty. Let's prove them wrong and liberate yourself from their bondage!

In the *Diving Deeper* section, I'll be guiding you through a few inner reflection exercises designed to help you get the facts you need to prove your mindset blocks wrong and ease your inner protector. The key here is to remain objective, real, and optimistic. The truth can convince your inner protector you're heading in the right direction. Facts can help you triumph over your fears. As you face your insecurities and give yourself a chance to

> As you face your insecurities and give yourself a chance to try, your self-confidence will strengthen.

try, your self-confidence will strengthen. Consequently, your inner critic will have less leverage to undermine your efforts. As you go through the questions and exercises, you'll be able to identify and document the truths and facts that will serve as your proof and motivator.

It's a time to challenge your unhealthy beliefs. Maybe you've adopted the harmful starving artist mentality. Perhaps you've believed you won't make it as a creative because you've been told by loved ones a career in art or any creative area is not a real career. Considering these words came from loved ones, chances are you believed and internalized them. You tried to rationalize this message and justified their intentions. *After all, they're loved ones and truly care about my well-being.* You stopped believing in yourself as a creative professional or as an artist. You stopped believing in your art. You simply stopped believing. *What if they're right? What if I won't make it as an artist?*

Maybe you didn't know or consider that, like any other career, there are professional development programs, coaches, and support systems that can help you take your art career to the next level and succeed. Perhaps you only knew your craft but lacked the knowledge necessary to convert your creative skill into a sustainable career. Supposed you could join a professional development support system like the Art NXT Level Academy that can help you strengthen your confidence and move your art career forward. Once you take the time to search and consequently find help, you'll realize your art can be a sustainable business.

As you prove to yourself that your blocks and self-sabotaging thoughts are not real, you will free yourself from these false and vicious assumptions. Let's think about this for a minute. What fact or facts do you have to prove your mindset block wrong? I invite you to pinpoint personal facts and interpersonal facts. Personal facts prove you can accomplish the goal you've set for yourself. In other words, facts show it is possible to achieve this goal. Some examples are your art career fulfills and inspires you, you do whatever is necessary to find time for your studio practice, you can create art, and you've prepared academically to become an artist.

Also, it's important to gather interpersonal facts. This is what others have been claiming about you as an artist and affirming your art. For instance, you posted an image of your art on social media, and most people reacted positively. Maybe others have told you repeatedly your work takes them into a state of calmness and peace. Perhaps you already have a space to make your art. Maybe professionals in the art world have expressed interest in exhibiting or selling your work, and strangers have purchased your art. Focus on what you have, not on what you wish you had, and use it to advance your goal. The key here is to take the time to identify your leverage. Don't take anything for granted!

The next step is to write a statement that proves your blocks or self-sabotaging thoughts wrong. This statement will state the actual truth about your capabilities and possible opportunities. Let me give you an example. Let's say you've been telling yourself, *I am incapable of succeeding in the art world.* Well, let's look at the facts. The facts are that you make art that matters, and you have the skills, knowledge, and experience exhibited in the art world. You're still trying to figure things out, but you're learning how to maneuver the art world. You also have shown your work in a few exhibitions and the number is growing. You're committing to taking action and advancing your art business. Therefore, your evidence is that you can be an artist based on your art background, experiences, and accomplishments. In addition, others have constantly been acknowledging how much they admire and appreciate your art. You may be facing challenges and hurdles, but they don't define who you are as an artist. You're capable of experiencing a successful art career if you commit to taking action.

Today, make it the day you no longer choose to allow your inner critic to sabotage your potential. You no longer let your inner protector keep you within your comfort zone, slow down your growth, or dictate your today and tomorrow. You've been experiencing these pressures for too long. It's time to create the change you want to see in your life. After reading this chapter, set time aside to answer the self-reflective questions under the *Diving Deeper* section. Once again, do not rush this exercise. You're doing serious inner work here, and it's essential you take your time to do it.

Sergio's Take

I love how Dr. Yanina helps us realize self-sabotage shows up precisely when we are about to make a decision that can positively impact our careers. I remember when I wanted to start a podcast for artists some years back. I had worked so hard on the concept, the name, the audience, the logo, and everything else. It was perfect! All I had to do was to get started. As soon as I took my idea seriously, immediately self-sabotaging thoughts started to creep into my head.

They said things like

- Sergio, English is your second language, and people are not going to like your accent.
- Other people have better podcasts than you do.
- Your voice sounds horrible on anything recorded.
- You do not know anything about podcasting. Why would people listen?

These voices were loud and clear. And in some way, they had some level of truth about me. English is indeed my second language. I learned English when I was sixteen years old, and therefore, I will always have some sort of accent. I do hate the sound of my voice on anything recorded up to this day. And yes, I did not know anything about podcasting, and resources were not as readily available as they are now.

As Dr. Yanina suggests in this chapter, I went back and took a hard look at the root of my insecurities. I soon realized the fear and the possibility of receiving negative criticism prevented me from moving forward on my goal. I did as Dr. Yanina suggested and proved these mindset blocks are guilty. First, I recognized personal facts. For example, yes, I do have an accent. I realized that was a good thing after all. It made me more recognizable and memorable. I also realized I had a message I wanted to share with people. Therefore, it did not matter if others had "better" podcasts. I found a coach I could hire to teach me all the technical aspects of running a successful podcast. Then, when others commented that I should start a podcast because they enjoyed how I explained things, well, that was an interpersonal fact right there in my face telling me I was on the right path.

After I made the mindset shift as a result of this exercise, I realized I could do it. It was a goal well worth pursuing. I acknowledged I had the potential to succeed if I focused more on what I had going for me than what I thought I had against me. What happened? Seven years, over 300 episodes published, tons of fabulous guests, and hundreds of thousands of downloads later, I now look back and see the success of *The Artist Next Level* podcast. Now I can see the results of what back then presented as a cloud of insecurities. Let me tell you, this exercise works! Your brain needs to experience a shift for you to believe in the possibilities ahead of you.

What is holding you back from your next goal? What are the voices you need to quiet by writing down your personal and interpersonal facts? Like mine, perhaps some of your insecurities have some grain of truth. I encourage you to take the time to complete the exercises recommended in this chapter to pass beyond your limiting beliefs.

Some of the most exciting success stories inside our artist coaching program are from artists who erroneously thought they could not create videos on Instagram, sell art online, build a website, market their art, get into important shows, build a sustainable career, and so on. Their outlook and enthusiasm for the future were clouded when their mind prevented them from achieving the goals they set for themselves. It feels liberating when you take hold of those thoughts and begin to experience the rewards of trusting in your facts.

Here is the deal: no matter what mindset blocks you are experiencing now—big or small—they can be put to rest. Even if you are going through a successful season where everything seems to be going fine, mindset blocks will eventually come. They always come and go. You will never get rid of them completely unless you stop pushing and challenging yourself. The only difference is now you have a tool to move forward and not get stuck. As you use the exercises in this chapter, it will become easier and easier to focus on the positive rather than the negative side of things.

Let's get to work and give yourself the gift of believing everything is possible.

Diving Deeper

If what if's, fears, doubts, and insecurities are distracting you from being productive and preventing you from maximizing your potential, it's time to identify, acknowledge and clear them so you can continue your journey. If you choose to ignore these blocks, you'll be holding yourself back from seeing the results you strive for as your mind is too busy worrying and wondering if you are doing the right thing.

1. Let's take a moment to acknowledge your blocks. Let's start with the strongest one. You can repeat this exercise with any other blocks.

    - What's my biggest mindset block right now? What's holding me back from achieving my goal or executing my plans?

      _____

      _____

    - What is the root of this block? How far back can you go to identify the first time you experienced this feeling? What happened?

      _____

      _____

    - What is preventing me from achieving this goal right now?

      _____

      _____

    - What circumstances are fueling this block or thought?

      _____

      _____

2. Now, let's prove them guilty! I encourage you to find facts to prove your mindset blocks wrong. Once you prove to yourself these mindset blocks are not real, you'll be able to free yourself from these false and vicious paralyzers.

- What fact(s) do I have to prove my mindset block *wrong?*
- Personal Facts (facts I have to prove I can accomplish this goal)

_____

_____

Interpersonal Facts (what others have been affirming about me and my work)

_____

_____

Here's a tip: Ask a friend, colleague, collector, or even a stranger looking at your artwork during an art opening night to share with you their response or reaction to your artwork. Each person brings their unique reaction to your artwork. Also, consider those who have written about your work.

- Based on the personal and interpersonal facts you have documented in this exercise, what is your conclusion? Write a statement that proves your block wrong by stating the actual evidence about your ability. Let's go over an example:

  o Mindset Block: "I am incapable of succeeding in the art world."
  o Facts: I have a world of experience and knowledge in the art world. People usually compliment my art, and I sell here and there.
  o Conclusion/Evidence: I can make art. I am committed to improving my art business. People often compliment my art and tell me

they experience a sense of calmness and peace when they look at my work. Also, I've been showing my work in exhibitions. Friends and people who don't know me have purchased my work.
- ○ Now it's your turn to identify yours.

- Write down your conclusion or evidence.
  _____
  _____
  _____
  _____

3. Let's Check In!

    How do you feel now that you've acknowledged and proved wrong the mindset block(s) that is sabotaging your potential and the results you want for yourself?

    I feel _____
    _____.

Wrapping It Up

You did it! You've taken the time to acknowledge and clear the mindset block that was crushing your potential. Doesn't it feel liberating? Each time you overcome a mindset block, you take a huge step closer to making your plans a reality. I hope you're feeling more confident and inspired to work harder. Remember, keep your eyes on the facts! Now that you are all clear, let's move on to Chapter Four: Freeing Myself from Negative Thinking.

CHAPTER FOUR
FREEING MYSELF FROM NEGATIVE THINKING

Welcome to Chapter Four! I'm so glad you're here! I would like to invite you to set the right tone for this chapter and create the atmosphere to help you safely focus and connect with your inner world. I recommend you sit or lie down comfortably, and have your sticky notes and pen or pencil ready. Of course, having your favorite coffee drink, hot tea, or water by your side adds to the greatness of the moment. I'm also drinking a hot double-expresso latte with honey, as I write this chapter. Turn on your favorite playlist as background music, and maybe light some incense or a few scented candles around the room. I want you to relax but not fall asleep. Make sure your bright lights are on. You can set up your perfect atmosphere each time you read this book. Now that you're in the zone, let's get started.

Have you ever met someone naturally optimistic who tends to see the glass half-full? It's crazy how they maintain a positive attitude and expect only good things to happen for them. These people are a rare human species inclined to choose hope and find an opportunity in every difficult situation. They are committed to finding goodness regardless of the circumstances surrounding them. Positive thinking comes naturally to them. For the sake of transparency, I'm not naturally optimistic. If you're anything like me, I have to work hard and be intentional about choosing optimistic thinking. Frankly, it can be quite challenging at times, especially when someone is speeding on the highway and, in a blink of an eye, cuts you off in traffic. I believe we can shift our negative thinking habits into optimistic, realistic thinking patterns. We can do this by being intentional about practicing optimistic thinking daily. I've found daily personal affirmations can help us rewire our thinking patterns. We can also shift a negative thought into a more optimistic one right on the spot.

In this chapter, I will share some of the causes behind negative thinking or cognitive distortions that happen to many of us. These distortions occur when your brain either lies to you or tricks you into believing something without considering facts. Yes, your brain can do that to you. What a traitor! Simply put, we're going to learn how to pin down those thoughts our brain creates to convince us of something when in reality, it's not true. You'll also learn how to identify your negative thinking habits and replace them with healthy ones. You'll become aware of common negative thinking traps so they don't affect your mental state, creativity, and willpower. Are you ready to dive into this issue together? Great! Buckle up now, my dear reader! It might be a bumpy ride, but it's worth it!

Let me start by saying many of us need help with optimistic thinking. There's no shame in that! Since we're here to take action and become the best version of ourselves, we're taking time to understand our thinking patterns. Our thoughts and values determine how we see ourselves and the world around us. Pessimistic thoughts and beliefs can negatively affect your feelings, emotions and physical and mental health. They can also hinder your ability to advance your creative career.

> Our thoughts and values determine how we see ourselves and the world around us.

Interestingly, your brain is programmed to remember and focus on unpleasant experiences more than pleasant ones. This dates back to the first humans who lived in the prehistoric era. It was a form of survival. If they wanted to survive, they had to remember negative situations and avoid hazardous areas, especially those where large hungry wild animals gathered. Simply put, dangers and threats were at the top of their heads so they could stay alive. That still holds today. We can also attribute this tendency to our attempt to cope with trauma and adverse life events. In other words, we adopt thinking patterns, whether healthy or toxic, that will increase our chance of survival.

Interestingly, we still retain negative information more than positive. For instance, say someone asks about your day. Would you likely share the problems and obstacles you faced first? Maybe you forget to mention that your friend stopped by your studio this morning, brought your favorite coffee drink or tea, and stayed a little while for a friendly chat. Perhaps you'll bring up right away the jerk who cut you in line at the grocery store or maybe the curator who said she was going to return your call today but didn't do so. Yet, you may forget to share how the new technique you've been trying so hard to improve worked out for you today. The problem with this tendency is it often gets in the way of your happiness, increases your stress level, hurts relationships, and affects your mental and physical wellness. After all, who wants to hang out with someone who is constantly a downer?

Keep in mind each of us experiences the world uniquely but also differently. You have your beliefs, memories, and attitudes about yourself, others, and the world. I have mine too. These are often influenced or shaped by our upbringing, education, religious or spiritual beliefs, and our life experiences.

Often, when we hold a self-sabotaging belief, hit a wall, or things don't go as planned, our minds tend to default to negative thinking instead of problem-solving. If you believe your identity is defined solely by the art you make, you can feel like the queen or king of the world as long as things are going well in your studio and with your art business. When you are faced with unforeseen setbacks or obstacles, such as your proposal for a solo exhibition being rejected, negative thinking patterns can lead you to overanalyze or exaggerate the severity of the situation. Your default conclusion may be, *I am a failure as an artist. There's no hope for my art career. What am I going to do now?*

As you feed this type of thinking, you ultimately welcome unnecessary anxiety in your life. The more you allow yourself to be carried away by negativity, the more you obstruct your perspective and the more labels you will put on yourself (*i.e.*, I'm a loser, a failure, not good enough, an impostor, *etc.*). That can hinder your self-esteem, deflate your self-confidence and even cause symptoms of depression. Consequently, the way you see the world and the labels you adopt will affect how you respond to the world and your relationships. It also creates a ripple effect in how you value and speak to yourself.

Your mind is very powerful. On the one hand, it can make decisions to improve the quality of your life. It can also adopt a growth and courageous mindset, present you with possibilities, heal your self-esteem, boost self-confidence, and improve the way you value and talk to yourself. In the same way, if you're not careful, your mind can also adopt a toxic way of thinking, present you with limits, distort the way you value and talk to yourself, and bombard you with self-criticism that only fuels your insecurities and fears. Did I mention your mind is very powerful?

Our personal beliefs, opinions, and values are learned over time. Some may become toxic habits as time passes. These thoughts are so ingrained in our brain that, often, we do not even realize it. Consciously or not, we allow our minds to fall into negative thinking traps. That's why we have to be aware of these traps and become intentional about avoiding and overcoming them. Once we identify our negative thinking patterns, we can fight self-brain-washing and pin down and change these toxic habits.

> Once we identify our negative thinking patterns, we can fight self-brain-washing and pin down and change these toxic habits.

Most importantly, you will have a mind that works for you and not against you. By no means I'm claiming the negative thinking traps I'm about to share with you are the only ones we can fall into. There are too many to cover in this chapter. I am sharing the most common traps I've seen creatives fall into so you can be proactive and avoid them.

Let's begin with the all-or-nothing thinking trap. If you only accept extremes and refuse to consider the possibilities in between, you've fallen for the all-or-nothing trap. Those struggling with this trap tend to use absolute terms such as always, nothing, every time, ever, or never. Consequently, they struggle to see alternatives and come up with possibilities in any given situation. Unfortunately, they focus on the downside to any given situation and adopt a black or white approach to decision-making. They think if they don't get a solo show, they will never be respected as an artist. Either your art is perfect or a disgrace. There's no in-between space for self-reflection, learning, and growing. Is it all-or-nothing for you?

When you fall into the mind-reading thinking trap, you assume you know what someone else is thinking. You may be so caught up in this way of thinking that you find asking for clarification or confirmation of something unnecessary. *He's probably thinking I'm not going to be accepted in the artist-in-residence program because my art is not on a par with his.*

When you make assumptions about other people, you're welcoming toxic thoughts that often are not even true. You're feeding your mind with false information and convincing yourself it is right. These thoughts can lead to more severe consequences if you're not careful. Another tendency of the mind-reading trap is expecting others to know what you think. *She should know I'm not interested. Why do I have to tell her?*

As you can imagine, making false assumptions about others and assuming others know your thoughts can certainly lead to misunderstandings and miscommunication. Are you upset with someone who didn't respond the way you expected because you thought, *they should know*? If so, this might be an area in need of your attention.

Do you believe you have the gift of predicting the future? Some people think they can predict negative outcomes without considering facts and possibilities. Don't misunderstand me. We can predict to some degree outcomes based on past experiences and our knowledge. For instance, if you have not learned how to swim, you can safely predict you'll drown if left behind in the middle of the ocean. You can also expect your art won't be selected if you don't follow the instructions and deadlines for a group exhibition to a tee. To a certain degree, this ability to predict the future is essential for survival. Those who fall into the fortune-telling and negative thinking traps believe their future is already set in stone but not in their favor. They tend to assume things will go wrong based on an assumption and not necessarily on facts or evidence. Sadly, they tend to predict turbulent circumstances and convince themselves misfortune is their destiny. In other words, they tend to think thoughts like, *why should I apply for this job position if others with more experience will also be applying for the same position?* Consequently, those stuck in this trap might miss out on amazing opportunities because they assume they don't deserve to succeed.

Have you ever encountered someone who tends to overgeneralize situations and therefore stops trying? They assume they will always experience the same negative results because it happened to them once. They think, *My relationship was a failure. Therefore, I will never be happy with another person.*

Perhaps you wrote an amazing exhibition proposal, submitted it to a local business, and it was rejected. Now you tend to overgeneralize your past results, believing your efforts will be dismissed each time you submit an exhibition proposal. Therefore, why bother?

Overgeneralization is another trap. We learn from past experiences and those of others. We learn from our mistakes and don't want to repeat them. No one wants to relive the pain and frustration caused by a past mistake. I understand. As you try to avoid possible frustration or pain, you may be depriving yourself of a second chance to experience success.

As we keep moving along the negative thinking trap highway, we find ourselves stumbling into the jumping-to-conclusions trap. It's so easy to jump to conclusions, especially when we want to blame others or protect ourselves. Drawing conclusions is not always wrong. You can conclude your friend has extraordinary culinary abilities. After visiting several art museums around the country and reading reviews on the internet, you can also conclude the best one is located in your hometown.

Those struggling with this thinking trap tend to draw negative conclusions with little or no evidence of their assumptions. When you fall into this trap, you find yourself arriving at negative conclusions again and again. You judge a situation, a person, or even deciding without having all the facts available. You find yourself rehearsing all negative possibilities. Consequently, your stress level goes through the roof, and your anxiety is out of control. As you may have guessed, mind-reading and fortune teller are variations of the jumping-to-conclusion thinking trap. Have you been catching yourself jumping to conclusions lately?

Picture this. An artist stops by a local gallery known for displaying art similar to his work. He introduces himself to the gallery owner. The owner thanks him for stopping by and tells the artist she's presently installing an upcoming show. Hence, she's quite busy and unable to speak with him at the moment. She asks the artist to leave his catalog and contact information on her desk. As she's walking him out, she tells the artist she will contact him when she has a moment. It's been two days, and the artist has not heard from the gallery owner. As a person who tends to fall into the jumping to conclusions trap, he may have thought, *It's been a couple of days, and I haven't heard from the gallery owner. She's probably blowing me off. Maybe my art is not good enough for her gallery. She's not going to call me back.* Does this situation resonate with you? If so, maybe this is an area that needs urgent intervention.

Let's take a moment to check in. How are you feeling right now? Are you discovering or confirming the traps into which you've been falling? Are you surprised about your self-discovery? You're welcome to write it down somewhere around this page or in your wellness journal. I'm the first to admit it can be quite overwhelming to become aware of these traps and how easily we can fall into them. It's probably consuming a lot of energy from you. My intention is not to overwhelm you but rather to guide you through the process of self-awareness. Change won't happen until we pinpoint the areas that need improvement. As we continue, I encourage you to identify the traps you're falling into so you can address them and eventually replace them with healthier thinking patterns.

Maybe now is a good time to stretch your body and refill your coffee, water, hot tea, or whatever you're drinking. When you're ready, let's move on to our next negative thinking trap, which is catastrophizing. This trap entices you to assume the worst will always happen. You tend to take things out of proportion and fixate on the worst possible results. You predict chaotic circumstances and may also believe you're incapable of dealing with the situation. As you get caught up in your story, you keep adding more and more catastrophic possibilities. You find yourself experiencing a series of intense, unpleasant emotions due to the story you're creating in your head with no evidence to support it. You're feeling exhausted, devastated, scared, and stressed out. I wouldn't be surprised if, at some point, you may find yourself on the merge of a panic attack.

He hasn't replied to my text message. He is probably angry and doesn't want to hear from me. Or maybe something horrible happened to him. Did he get into a car accident? That's a possibility. Oh no! Should I call 911? Maybe I should call the local hospitals.

If this trap tends to get you, where do you usually feel the pressure in your body? Write it down somewhere around this paragraph or in your journal. Next time you experience this sensation in your body, you know it's a trap! Use it as an incentive to crush this trap for good.

The last negative thinking trap I will cover in this chapter is minimizing yourself. When you fall into this trap, you label your abilities and potential inferior to others. You also label your achievements irrelevant or not a big deal. You keep telling yourself, *Sure, I'm an okay artist, but anyone can do better than me.* As you linger on this trap, you begin to doubt yourself and your abilities. You might even believe you're fooling others into believing you are an artist. You begin to experience the impostor phenomenon. As a result, you feel intimidated, insecure, and you lack confidence. If you feel like an impostor, you'll find Chapter Six valuable. In it, I dive into this phenomenon and teach you a few practical strategies to help you overcome it.

Frankly, there will always be someone better than you and someone less fortunate than you. At the end of the day, it's a mind game where you're either able to adopt the victim role or the hero role. When you minimize yourself and your art, others will not see a reason to support you. On the other hand, others will follow when you begin to respect your art and take pride in your work. My question to you is: What mindset are you going to adopt?

There's always light at the end of the tunnel—a rainbow after the storm. The good news is all negative habits can be unlearned. We can eliminate them from our lives if we choose to take action. Do not allow anyone to convince you otherwise. Take time to identify, unlearn, and replace your negative thinking patterns so your mind works for you and not against you.

When I intentionally changed my negative thinking patterns, I quickly noticed their potential for wreaking havoc. I decided to do something about it. As I was doing my inner work, I noticed I began to follow a pattern or formula. Simply put, you're discarding the thought of your mind symbolically. Without further ado, let me share with you my formula to crushing negative thinking:

STOP + LABEL + TOSS + REPLACE = HEALTHIER THINKING

Before using this formula, you have to make yourself aware of your negative thinking habits. In the *Diving Deeper* section, you'll be able to pinpoint your most common habits. This will help you create self-awareness and, consequently, help you catch yourself right away. I would like to share this visual imagery exercise that has been helping me and others whom I have taught to transfer these thoughts from your inner realm into the outer realm. Are you ready to do this exercise with me? Excellent!

Once your mind produces a negative thought, immediately stop yourself. Next, label the thought as toxic immediately. Tell yourself, *This thought is toxic and unwelcomed.* Whether you speak the thought out loud or in your head, address it the same way. What's important is you stop yourself and label it as toxic. No one wants to linger around toxicity. Since anything toxic is unpleasant and dangerous, the first reaction is to get rid of it or toss it away. Right? That's why it's important to label your negative thought as toxic. No shame or put-downs allowed!

Next, I want you to imagine a trash can. It can be a small trash can, a tall trash can, or a dumpster. It's your call. You're going to toss the toxic thought into the trash can. As you do this, you're sending your mind the message that this thought is no good, unwelcome, and unnecessary. You want to get it out of your head and dispose of it. The next step is to replace the thought with a positive and more realistic thought. Once again, do this right on the spot. As you repeat this formula, it'll become your default reaction. The best part is you'll begin to adopt healthier thinking. You're going to be unlearning negative habits while training your brain to be more optimistic, hopeful, and realistic. Follow this formula each time your mind lingers toward a negative thinking trap.

Keep in mind that, like any new habit, it will take some time for your mind to change the unhealthy thinking pattern. Remember, you have to unlearn this pattern that has been ingrained in your brain and replace it with healthier thoughts. It's going to take time, energy, and effort to make it happen. See it as a cleansing process. You're going to make mistakes. It's okay! There's no need for shame, harshness, or self-guilt. On the contrary, this is when you choose to bombard yourself with grace, self-compassion, a tremendous amount of patience, and repetition.

For each negative thinking trap I discuss in this chapter, I'm going to share with you one or two things you can do to unlearn it and avoid falling into each specific trap ever again. I'm also sharing a few tips to help you replace negativity with a more productive way of thinking. This is not the time to put off the work you've been doing in this chapter. Stay here; you can do this! Let's keep going.

As we did with our mindset blocks and self-sabotage, we will challenge our unhealthy thoughts. You want to prove to yourself and your protectors those thoughts are no longer welcome in your inner world.

As you recall, all-or-nothing thinking is notorious for its use of absolute words and taking things to extremes. An all-or-nothing person might say, "Since I always mess up the opportunities that come my way, I will never make it as an artist."

If this is a trap you've been struggling with, I invite you to reset your mindset by labeling unpleasant or unwanted outcomes as learning experiences instead of failures. When you label an outcome as a learning experience, the message you're telling yourself is there's space for improvement and change. There's an opportunity for redemption. Your future is not set in stone. In other words, your past does not define your present or your future. The actions you take and the decisions you make today will determine your future. Rather than asking yourself, *why should I try again if I always ruin everything*? decide instead that simply because it didn't work out previously, it won't stop you from figuring things out. Many things can go wrong in life. Remind yourself that because things go wrong once, it doesn't mean it will always be that way. Consider your options, learn from past experiences, don't repeat mistakes, ask for advice, and you'll be better able to make wiser decisions for yourself and your creative career.

I have news for you, if you tend to fall into the mind-reading trap. Admit it. You know you can't read people's minds. You can make all the assumptions you want and react based on these unfounded assumptions. Yet, you're only hurting relationships and scaring people away. I invite you to practice self-awareness instead of falling into this toxic pattern,. Take some time to reflect on the reasons why you tend to make assumptions about others. Could it be a bias or a stereotype has infiltrated your thinking? Could it be an experience you have generalized has become a belief? Or perhaps, it was a belief t you were taught growing up, and now you're going with the flow.

As you become more aware of this tendency, be intentional about catching yourself and correcting your thoughts right away. Use my formula to crushing negative thinking:

STOP + LABEL + TOSS + REPLACE

Tell yourself, *I cannot read the minds of others. I'm not going to assume what I don't know.* Before making assumptions about others, ask them to clarify what they think and feel. It's important you communicate clearly and accurately. There's always a chance you may be wrong or you're jumping to conclusions without having the complete picture. For your peace of mind and the sake of your relationships, keep working on overcoming this thinking pattern.

By now, you know the fortune-telling trap is a destroyer of aspiration and ambition. If you think this way, I invite you to explore the reasons why you tend to default to negative predictions. Are these circumstances triggering fear or insecurities? I challenge you to question your belief. Like any mindset block, you want to prove this belief wrong. One way is asking yourself what evidence you have that proves the belief is correct or wrong?

When this type of thinking pops on your head, immediately replace it with a thought that awakens possibilities. Don't predict you won't make it as an artist; replace it with this statement instead: *No one can predict the future, including me. I'm making assumptions, and it is unhealthy. I will take action toward growing my creative business and expect great outcomes.* It's a mindset. When you're constantly feeding your mind with possibilities, even when you doubt yourself, you'll eventually convince yourself you can indeed succeed in what you do. If you're experiencing self-doubt, start pretending you believe in yourself. You can do this by telling yourself it is possible. Say it again and again until you believe it. Print it on paper or write it on a sticky note. Post it on your bedroom and bathroom mirrors so you can see it every day. Like any new habit, it's going to take some repetition before you adopt this new way of thinking. An effective way to convince yourself you deserve to live a fulfilling life is through personal affirmations. In Chapter Five, I'll share steps you can follow to write your personal affirmation.

If overgeneralization has kept you away from trying new things in your creative career or personal growth, think twice. It's smart to learn from your mistakes so you don't repeat them. Like the proverb says, "Fool me once, shame on you. Fool me twice, shame on me." You may be depriving yourself of an amazing opportunity because you generalize outcomes based on past experiences. Keep in mind that time changes people. Some people choose to change for the better, and others for the worse. The rest decide not to change at all. In your case, you're changing for the better. Time can bring maturity, wisdom, experience, and opportunities.

Have you considered the possibility you were not ready the first time you tried? Maybe you needed more experience or a better understanding of how things work. Perhaps you were too young and lacked the maturity to take on responsibilities, or you weren't ready for the opportunity. Possibly it was not the right time or the right place. As time passes, we acquire the experience and maturity we need to make better choices. We also equip ourselves with the tools we need to overcome the difficulties life throws at us. Don't underestimate your potential even when you failed in the past. Simply because your past decisions and results were not what you planned or expected, it doesn't mean you aren't ready today. Try again! Don't rob yourself of opportunities because things didn't turn out as planned in the past. Today is a new day filled with new possibilities, should you take steps to turn your aspirations into reality.

> Don't underestimate your potential even when you failed in the past.

If the jump-to-conclusions trap is destroying relationships and opportunities for you, it's time to do something about it. By now, you've realized this trap taps into your insecurities, biases, and fears. Often, conclusions based on this way of thinking are false or merely assumptions. Unfortunately, you end up labeling and avoiding others and feeling hopeless and frustrated. You believe the result will be negative, people can't be trusted, and default on judging others.

Again, when you catch yourself speculating with little or no facts, use my formula to crush negative thinking. As a reminder, it is **STOP + LABEL + TOSS + REPLACE**.

Self-awareness is important here to catch yourself and stop making unfounded conclusions.

Before jumping to conclusions about your art career, write down the possibilities available to you. Write down those opportunities not available to you yet but that you can start exploring now. Claim what you have and manifest what you don't have yet. Rather than thinking, *Probably the gallery owner is ignoring my calls because my art is not good enough*, consider removing the spotlight off yourself. Maybe you can conclude you will follow up if you don't hear from her in a couple of days. Presume she is very busy with the upcoming show, and returning your call is certainly not the only item on her agenda.

Another exercise you can try is writing down your conclusion or story. This will help you create imagery where you detach yourself from the story and remove it from your head so you can see it from an outsider's perspective. The story is no longer in your head, but it's now on a piece of paper or electronic device. Next, write down the emotions emerging from this conclusion. Once you have the story written and the emotions associated with this story, ask yourself, *What's bothering me here? Is it personal biases or fear? Is this story true, or am I distorting it to justify or cover up my insecurities?*

As you reflect on what's happening in your inner world, you'll be able to identify speculations and replace your distortion with facts. You always want to have outside evidence or facts to support your conclusion. We'll continue the inner work in the *Diving Deeper* section below.

All right, let's talk about the catastrophizing thinking trap. I would like to acknowledge that coming up with worst-case scenarios over and over can be quite exhausting. You end up working yourself up into a bit of a state. We all experience some fear and worry in our lives. It's part of being a human. I am talking about constantly fearing the worst and falling into a tragic mode without having the facts. The good news is you can catch yourself at the onset and snap out of it or fully avoid the catastrophizing thinking trap. How? Excellent question! Take action toward finding solutions for the situation you're facing instead of focusing on possible adverse outcomes. Conceptualize a positive outcome or even a less-negative option. The moment you catch yourself blowing the problem out of proportion, stop yourself right away and tell yourself, *I'm overstating or exaggerating. Is this a toxic thought? A more helpful or useful way to see this is _____.*" Then create a more positive scenario.

Like the jump-to-conclusions thinking trap, don't allow your negative story to become the headlines for the evening local news. This is crucial, especially when you don't have all the facts at hand. I can't encourage you enough to replace your story with a more optimistic and realistic one. *He did not reply to my text message. He is probably busy or unable to talk at the moment. It has nothing to do with me. He'll answer when he has time.*

The minimizing yourself negative thinking trap has deeper roots. It is a reaction to unresolved inner conflicts often associated with traumatic experiences. They usually manifest as insecurities, low self-esteem, and lack of confidence. Self-sabotage and mindset blocks are examples of what you will encounter when you fall into this trap. If you're finding yourself refuting compliments from others, invalidating your efforts, accomplishments and putting your skills down, maybe this is an area that needs your immediate attention. If you continue on this path, you'll find yourself becoming more insecure, dissatisfied, and living an unfulfilling life. Your way of thinking will lead to self-imposed limitations and feeling defeated. I know you don't want that lifestyle for yourself. Not at all!

Let me share a powerful strategy I've been teaching people to crush this trap. It's not the only strategy, but it's so simple and easy it works. When someone takes the time to compliment you, simply say, "Thank you, I appreciate it." Say it even if you assume they don't mean it. Stop the urge to justify or minimize the compliment. Don't allow your thoughts to wander off and sabotage the moment. Avoid the urge to justify their complements. "I got lucky about being in this exhibition. I don't even understand why they chose my work considering the caliber of the works in this show."

Once again, you don't need to justify anything. Say, "Thank you, I appreciate it." That's it! The fact is no one is obligated to compliment you. Seriously! Most times, if someone compliments you or acknowledges your efforts, it is likely because they mean it. If you reject their compliment, you're minimizing yourself, and you're also hurting their feelings or even insulting them. You're suggesting or sending the message that they're either lying, faking, pretending, or being dishonest. Yes, a few people compliment others for selfish reasons, but most people mean what they say.

What if I feel like or am perceived as a show-off? Excellent question! There's a big difference between being conceited and being grateful. Each of us was created with unique abilities and gifts. As time goes by, we develop our skills and acquire new ones. We educate ourselves, learn from experiences and gain wisdom. We all have strengths and weaknesses. We work hard and relentlessly for what we have acquired, whether it is a position, knowledge, or recognition. Acknowledging your strengths and accomplishments doesn't make you prideful or selfish. It makes you aware of who you truly are and what you have. It makes you confident and fierce. The effect of welcoming other people's compliments goes above and beyond this limited assumption. As you begin to accept your abilities, you'll start to experience a stronger sense of self, greater peace of mind, and fulfilling life.

It's crucial you pin down this issue now. I'm so serious about this invitation that I wrote an entire chapter to address self-trust. I encourage you to check out Chapter Six in this book to learn more powerful ways to build and maintain self-trust and confidence. I would like to see you telling yourself, *I can improve myself and grow my business. I sometimes make mistakes, and it's okay. Every day I am taking steps to become a better and more confident person.*

Make sure you take time to do your inner work in the *Diving Deeper* section at the end of this chapter. But, before you do, check out *Sergio's Take* below. I'm sure you'll feel inspired and motivated to make the necessary changes in your life for the best.

Sergio's Take

Generalization is one of the thinking traps I have often caught myself falling into. It is something I have to be aware of and remind myself to stop, label, toss, and release. In 2009, I saw an opportunity to launch my curatorial career on a national stage. After five years of curating shows in our small gallery, I conceptualized an idea for a larger national show. I wanted to curate a big exhibition to bring the top painting MFA students to Chicago from the most respected graduate programs in the United States. The goal was to investigate what graduate programs were proposing in the medium of painting. I wanted to celebrate painting and investigate these two questions:

- Is painting still alive and relevant in the American MFA programs?

- Are emerging artists looking for new ways to explore what a painting is?

    I called the concept the National Wet Paint MFA Exhibition. Although I had seen many MFA shows, I had never seen one dedicated to only the medium of painting at a national scale.

The idea was solid, but the challenges ahead of me were intimidating. I needed ample gallery space, a team of people, contacts to all graduate programs, and financial support because I did not want to make it into a pay-for-play type of show. It had to be free of charge for the students to submit and participate if they were selected for the show. I did not want money to get in the way of a talented graduate student to participate. I still remember the moment I realized the complexity of the job I was about to get into if I pursued this idea. My mind began to accentuate the obstacles by generalizing ideas in my head. The first thoughts that came to mind were things like, *nobody will give me a large space as a new curator,* or *no one will trust or listen to me.* The worst of all was, *no graduate program is going to participate.* I started to fall into these generalizations and negative thinking patterns. Every time I was about to start moving forward with my idea, one of these generalizations would stop me from moving forward.

Have you ever experienced similar negative thinking patterns? Perhaps with a proposal you want to send out, a collaboration you want to be part of, a patron you want to ask for support, a gallery or curator you want to approach, or a residency program where you want to apply. You get caught in the same negative thinking trap I did. They are real, and sometimes they have a grain of truth. Otherwise, we would not consider them a possibility, but more often than not, we put the word "no" in the other person's response without even giving them a chance to answer for themselves. We make false assumptions and steal their opportunity to decide whether they want to buy into our idea. I believe this particular problem has robbed thousands of artists of a shot at great opportunities. After all, if you do not ask, most of the time, you do not get. I have come to believe I do not want to steal someone else's chance to say yes or no. Therefore, I must keep asking. I know it is a mindset game, but it works for me.

Back to my story. I remember sharing this big exhibition idea with Dr. Yanina and going over the various negative scenarios inside my head. I do not recall the details of our conversations, but I know for sure they gave me the confidence I needed to give it at least a shot. I am sure we went into some stop, label, toss, and release exercise that gave me the tools to begin the process. After all, this would be the type of event that would launch my curatorial career or perhaps burn it from the start, and I would make a fool of myself. The stakes were that high for me.

To make a long story short, this is how I started replacing negative thinking traps with practical action steps. Each step had to find a *yes* to continue with the next one. First, I took the time to write a compelling proposal for my project. Second, I presented my proposal to the Zhou Brothers, who were the first to say yes. They were internationally recognized artists who founded the Zhou B Art Center, where I was a member. It had a beautiful and enormous gallery space to host the exhibition. Once that was a yes, I put together a team of interns. We worked for weeks, gathering contacts from all the MFA programs around the country. Once that was finished, we sent invitations, emails letters, and made phone calls about the show. To my surprise, the response was overwhelming, and many MFA programs started to say yes to spreading the word to their graduate students. In some cases, they offered to pay for the shipping of the artwork to Chicago.

On a cold January 15, a Friday evening, we opened the doors of the first National Wet Paint MFA Exhibition with the participation of over forty MFA programs from around the country. It was the start of an amazing project. Each year, the exhibition became larger and more difficult to get in. After many exciting exhibitions and hundreds of emerging artists participating, we decided to end it in 2018 and move on to other new projects.

Looking back, the National Wet Paint MFA Exhibition has been one of the most rewarding curatorial projects of my career. What if I had believed the negative thoughts and felt for the patterns stirring inside my head? What if I had not given the people I approached with my idea a chance to say yes or no? Not everyone said yes, but I did not give up. I was lucky to find enough people who said yes along the way. I wonder how many yeses are waiting for you if you only ask. I wonder what doors you need to knock on today, this week, or this month to get the yes that can change everything. Maybe you have believed no one is ever going to say yes. That is exactly what generalization is all about. Do not allow yourself to get stuck with any of the negative thinking patterns Dr. Yanina has shared in this chapter. Perhaps you do not have a supporting partner and psychologist as I do in Dr. Yanina, but now you have this book and this new mantra to help you: **STOP + LABEL + TOSS + REPLACE**. Own it and practice it in your art career. It will change your life as it has changed mine.

Diving Deeper

Are you ready to crush the negative thinking habits that mess up your head and sabotage your life? I heard you say yes. So, let's get to work. I'm going to share four steps you can take to replace negativity with a more optimistic way of thinking and living your life.

Step 1. Self-awareness.

- Which of these negative thinking traps do you tend to experience?
  _____
  _____

- What circumstances tend to trigger this trap? Remember, awareness is an essential step toward change.
  _____
  _____

Step 2. Pick a negative habit or thought lingering in your head right now and you want to unlearn.

- Write it down.
  _____
  _____

- Next, cross it out and label it as *toxic*.
  _____
  _____

- Write it again, but this time replace it using a more positive and realistic approach. Your sentence below is what you're going to tell yourself next time this negative habit or thought pops in your head.
  _____
  _____

Step 3. Write a letter to your best friend.

When we make a mistake or get unwanted results, we often react cruelly and harshly toward ourselves. We don't comfort and encourage ourselves to correct our mistakes and learn from them; we usually do the opposite. We put ourselves down. The result is we feel defeated. By now, you've learned this approach is not helpful at all. If we want to grow and succeed, we have to practice self-compassion and self-forgiveness and be willing to improve our lives.

The truth is, you would probably never talk to your closest friend the way you speak to yourself the same way you would toward your friend if they came to you for advice and encouragement. You deserve to be kind to yourself. This exercise will help support yourself in the same way you would a friend.

When your mind turns to toxic thinking, including self-sabotage, follow these steps:

Step One. Write your negative thought in your journal.

_____

_____

Step Two. Imagine this thought is something your friend is experiencing and has shared with you.

_____

_____

Step Three. Think of words of encouragement you would tell your friend to lift their spirits.

_____

_____

Step Four. Write a letter of encouragement as if you were writing it to your friend. Surprise! This letter is for you. Read it over and over again until it becomes your words.

It's time you begin talking to yourself the same way you would to your best friend.

Step Five. Adopt a healthier lifestyle. Negativity tends to consume our mental and physical energy. As we work toward unlearning unwanted habits and learning healthier ones, we have to care for ourselves. If we don't, our inner-tank will be emptied. When that happens, we are at risk of physical and mental collapse. We have to do what we can to avoid this tragedy.

- Which health habits need your attention right now to experience healthy living? Some examples are annual physical exams, exercise, eating habits, sleep, me time, and emotional or psychological wellness.

- Which mental relaxation exercises can you start practicing to experience peace of mind, calmness, and wholeness? Examples are guided meditation, breathing exercises, tapping (emotional freedom technique), reiki, yoga, connecting with your spirituality through prayer, Zen sand gardens, and aromatherapy.

Wrapping It Up

Do you want to go deeper in your healing journey? Repeat these exercises as needed.

Before you move to the next chapter, take some time to acknowledge and celebrate the wins you've acquired in this chapter. You've worked so hard, and you deserve to celebrate your growth. Share your wins with your significant other or a close friend who respects your efforts. As a reminder, you can invite them to be your accountability partner and join you in your journey. You can check in with them after completing each chapter and go over the areas you commit to change. Allow them to remind you gently to discard toxic thoughts or use the formula if they witness you falling into a trap.

In the next chapter, we're going to create a plan of action that will help you identify areas in your life that need to be let go of and acknowledge those helping you move forward. See you in Chapter Five!

PART TWO
LIVING FULLY AND CREATING WITH PURPOSE

CHAPTER FIVE
GETTING ORGANIZED AND MAKING THINGS HAPPEN

If I were to pick one question people ask Sergio again and again, it's this: "How can you get so many things done in one day considering all you do as an artist, gallery owner, art curator, artist coach, and a family man? You organize exhibitions, are very active on social media, constantly promote your art, and share valuable information with artists through your podcast, show, etc. How on earth can you do it all? Do you ever sleep?"

The answer is focus and organization (and yes, a good night's sleep)!

In my experience, one of the most common challenges artists keep bringing up is the ongoing struggle with organization, which affects planning and accomplishing their goals. They want to succeed in their art career yet, often, they find themselves struggling with organization and getting things done. As a result, many feel unmotivated and frustrated. Some simply go with the flow and hope for the best.

"I'm so unorganized when it comes to the business side of my art practice. I don't even know where to start. I wish I only have to focus on making art and have someone else take care of the rest!" some say. Frankly, the struggle is real! Do you know what is also real and more meaningful? Your passion, purpose, goals, growth, and plans. Do not let this struggle distract you from what truly matters to you.

Many years ago, before Sergio and I got married, he invited me to a local restaurant for a date night. We had a delightful time and a delicious dinner. When the time came to pay the check, Sergio pulled out a stack of bills from his jeans back pocket. Not from a wallet, but from his pocket!

As someone who opened her bank account when I was a teenager, I was shocked when I saw that stunt. "How can you carry all those bills in your pocket? Isn't it uncomfortable? Don't you have a bank account?" I asked him.

With no shame, he said to me, "No I don't. I haven't found the need to open a bank account yet."

"Have you ever lost money for carrying it in your jeans?" I asked.

"Yes, I have," he answered.

When we got married, guess what was one of the first things we took care of right away? You guessed it right. We opened a joint bank account. Interestingly, I noticed most things related to his art practice were a bit of a mess too. Let me cut him some slack. By then, he was full-time art faculty at a local college, making art, starting an art gallery in Chicago, and getting involved in other art-related efforts in the Chicago area and abroad. He struggled with keeping up with deadlines, organizing his inventory, meeting some of the gallery's demands, and finding important things. At that point, I noticed he needed an intervention! As you can imagine, organization was the key to making things happen for him. Unless he became better organized, his art career, business, job, and overall wellness were at risk of collapsing. We got together, brainstormed possibilities, and listed those not so great habits that had to go. We also identified essential organizational skills and developed a strategy and a monitoring system to track his progress. We tried this system again and again. We kept tweaking, improving, and updating it until we found the one that worked best for him. We are still using the same system.

Of course, we didn't want to keep this system to ourselves. Once Sergio and I opened the doors of the Art NXT Level Academy, we began to teach thousands of artists how to stay organized amid ongoing distractions, create an effective plan of action, and implement a system to get things done. We called it *The Goal Setting and Progress System for Artists*. It has been helping thousands of artists from all over the world get organized, create a plan of action, monitor their progress, and achieve their goals practically and effectively. These artists are experiencing amazing results as they learn how to eliminate a few unhealthy habits that are holding them back and replace them with effective ones.

The point I'm trying to make is we all can learn to be organized and get things done. When people are astonished by how much Sergio can accomplish in his art career despite all his responsibilities and engagements, what they don't know is that he was not born this way. He had to do the hard work and learn to be organized to move his art career forward successfully. He had to unlearn a few unhealthy habits and get organized to make things happen for him.

On a side note, as you begin your journey toward becoming better organized and focusing on getting things done in your art career, it's important you also consider your physical and emotional state as a possible contributor to this struggle. Keep in mind that some people experience poor organizational skills and lack of attention and focus due to physical, neurological, or psychological deficiencies. Some examples are a poor diet, lack of rest, mental health disorders, and executive functioning problems including attention deficit disorder. Don't shy away from ruling out or addressing any physiological or psychological deficits that may be hindering your ability to concentrate, execute tasks, and complete projects or goals. It's important you cover all bases to set yourself up for success and get things done.

If you consider yourself one of the most disorganized people in the world, I have good news for you. There's still hope for you! Remember, not everyone is born with organizational skills. As you see, even the most organized people in the world today experienced turbulent beginnings (like Sergio). By the way, don't worry about our marriage. I won't be sent to the dog's house today for sharing Sergio's story in this chapter. He's the one who suggested I share it with you. We hope it sparks your motivation and you feel encouraged to do something about it.

Speaking of stories, you may have heard about a very small number of people who have experienced success without having an organized bone in their bodies. Others don't even have a plan of action in place, yet they seem to be moving on in their creative career. They simply go with the flow, and things simply happen for them. Similarly, you might have also heard about very few people who have become overnight art celebrities. Note that I emphasized this is true for a very, very few people.

Let's be honest with ourselves. We know this outcome is very rare. It's so rare we would be fooling ourselves if we generalize it and assume it will happen to us too. There's nothing wrong with being optimistic as long as you remain realistic. Frankly, most of us need to be organized, have a plan of action to accomplish our goals, and monitor our progress if we want to experience personal and professional growth. We have to invest in our development.

If you're struggling with getting things done in your art practice, this chapter is going to come in handy. I'm sharing four steps of *The Goal Setting and Progress System for Artists* course Sergio and I created. I'm also sharing how personal affirmations can help you stay focused on what truly matters. In the *Diving Deeper* section below, I'll be guiding you to write your personal affirmation. So, my dear reader, make sure you have your sticky notes and journal handy and pen or pencil ready. Let's get to work on this essential area in your personal growth!

There are many things you can do to get organized and make things happen for yourself. I'm narrowing it down to four manageable steps. The first step to getting organized and making things happen for you is to have a clear mind. In other words, you've got to have a clear vision of what direction you're heading or what you want to accomplish. Randomness and leaving things to chance only leads to confusion, unnecessary roadblocks, and feeling lost. Before you pack and take a vacation, you first decide your destination. You can't board an airplane scheduled to arrive in San Juan, Puerto Rico, change your mind while you're on air flying toward that destination, and ask the pilot to change its course because now you want to go to Barcelona, Spain.

If you want to arrive somewhere in life, you need clarity. Some people seem to have a clear idea of their destination, whereas others are still trying

If you want to arrive somewhere in life, you need clarity.

to figure it out. If you identify with the latter, there's no need to fret! We all start somewhere. Maybe your destination is not clear right now. That's okay. Some people need time to figure things out, and clarity happens as they embark on their journey. Others know what they want and how to get there from the beginning. If you haven't done so yet, now is the time to figure out what you want to accomplish as a creative or in your business.

Understand that as you're working on identifying and refining your destination or goals, your focus or purpose may shift, change, or evolve. What seems to be your ultimate goal or destination right now may change as you work toward accomplishing it. That is okay, as long as you stay true to what you want to accomplish. For instance, your goal may be to increase exposure and recognition. To achieve this goal, you create a plan for a solo exhibition at a local gallery or museum with a time frame of one to two years. As you're working toward achieving this goal, you may encounter other opportunities that are not necessarily a solo exhibition. yet they align with your plan. An example is a gallery that offers to represent your work in a prestigious international art fair booth.

Clarity is very important. Remember, you won't arrive at your optimal destination until you're clear about where you are going. See your goals as destination points. Once you're clear where you're heading, you'll be able to focus on how you will get there.

I would venture to say you want to accomplish many things in your creative career or business. Maybe you need a new website or a catalog that features your work. Perhaps you want to participate in a prestigious artist residence or write an exhibition proposal. *So many things to do, so little time*, you tell yourself. Usually, people create a never-ending list of everything they want to do. The problem with these lists is they are long and can be overwhelming. As you're reviewing your list, your head probably begins to twist around, which triggers your stress, and your motivation goes down the drain. Right?

Don't write an endless to-do list of everything that needs to be done to arrive at your destination. Let's break things down into more manageable tasks. Before we continue, let's step back for a second and make sure you've already defined what you want to see happening in your art career in six months or one year. You can go as far ahead as two years. Next, identify one or two sub-goals or tasks that will help you start the journey and make a difference in your personal life or art business right now. In other words, focus on one or two main steps you can take and start working on right now that will get you closer to your destination.

Keep in mind you can't do everything at once. Frankly, good planning involves intentional consecutive action steps where completing one task leads to taking the next step. There are times when an action step cannot be taken until an essential step is completed first. That is why it's so important you take the time to create a plan. Before you begin a new body of work, you must have your tools and materials available. Then, you have to schedule time in your studio to make the art. You cannot complete a new series of art unless you follow these necessary steps first.

There are roads to take, stops to make, and sometimes detours that force us to recalculate our route to any destination. The same happens during your journey toward achieving greatness in your creative career. Always keep in mind that as you embark on this journey, you will encounter situations you can control and others that are out of your control. Label the situations you cannot control as roadblocks and detours. Recalculate your route, and keep moving forward as you would if you were on a road trip.

Flexibility and self-compassion will come in handy when you face these types of hurdles in your journey. As much as we want to, we cannot control everything in our journey. It's okay to let go of the need to be in control and allow space for inner peace. Always set goals that push you beyond your comfort zone, make you feel a bit uncomfortable, and will lead to growth. Yes, your goals should be challenging.

Now that you have a good idea of your destination, let's move on to step two, which is to create a plan. Nothing gets done unless we take action. Planning will help you stay organized and focused. I'm not suggesting you pretend to be busy yet accomplish nothing. I'm talking about assigning yourself intentional and purposeful tasks. In my experience, the more intentional and prepared I am, the more I can accomplish in less time. In the *Diving Deeper* section below, you'll be writing down immediate action steps or tasks to help you kick start the journey toward achieving your personal and business-main goals.

Let's get practical here. There are a few things to consider as you begin to identify what needs to be done to achieve your goal. Do you need to research a specific area in your career, business, or personal development before you can take on this journey? Do you need to learn new skills or perhaps focus on fine-tuning your artistic abilities? Maybe you need to hire someone to help you in the studio, technology, or design support. Perhaps you have to grow your network or social media followers as a marketing strategy before you begin to create a sales plan. Perhaps, you have to unlearn toxic habits to make space for healthier ones.

Continuing with the increase recognition and exposure example, let's focus on finding exhibition opportunities for a solo show. In this step, you need to identify one or two immediate action steps that will kick start your journey and make a strong impact toward achieving this goal. Your first action step may be to begin your research on possible opportunities and venues open to accepting exhibition proposals. Your second action step is to write an exhibition proposal to send to the venues you have selected. Both action steps are challenging, possible, and necessary to accomplish this goal.

Once you have identified the initial action steps, assign a deadline to each, so they get done. It's important to respect your deadlines and avoid falling into the toxic procrastination trap at all costs. Time is precious and cannot be regained once it's gone. Like any type of currency, time is a valuable asset. You would never waste millions of dollars due to procrastination. Similarly, don't waste millions of minutes or seconds of your valuable time due to procrastination. It will destroy your hopes, dreams, and aspirations. As a reminder, life can be playful and throw situations at you that are out of your control. Delays may happen along the way. During these circumstances, be flexible, practice self-compassion, and be patient.

Finally, identify the resources and tools you'll need for each specific step. A sample list may look like this:

Action Step #1. Begin research on possible opportunities and venues open to accepting exhibition proposals.

- Tap into your professional network for possible contacts.
- Make a list of contact names with email or postal addresses.
- Search online listings for exhibition opportunities.

Action Step #2. Write an exhibition proposal

- Take a course to learn how to create a solid exhibition proposal.
- Budget to address possible expenses related to this goal.
- Update your portfolio.
- Obtain professional photographs of my art.

At this point, you're ready to move on to step three, which is accountability and progress tracking. As I suggested in the Introduction, partnering with an artist friend or trusted person to work with you on this book can be very helpful. If you haven't done so yet, I encourage you to invite someone to become your accountability partner. Get together with them to share your destination, action steps, and deadlines. Decide among yourselves how you can help each other stay focused and on track.

Next, I encourage you to track your progress. You may be asking why. Excellent question! If you're like me, I need to see my progress concretely. When I don't document or keep track of my progress, I tend to minimize, miss, or ignore my small wins. If we don't keep track of our accomplishments, especially the small ones, we may assume we aren't making any progress. This practice helps you stay on track, and you're able to catch yourself when you're slacking or falling behind. As distractions begin to sidetrack you from your destination, the practice of keeping track of your actions helps you stay focused so you avoid falling behind or putting things off.

As you see, there are many amazing benefits to keeping track of your progress. You're welcome to use the Monthly Goal Progress Tracking Chart Sergio developed, which we have included in this book. You can also use it as a sample to create your very own progress tracking chart. Post it in your studio, office, or somewhere you can see it daily. Always celebrate your wins, no matter how small.

Let's take a moment to check in before we keep going. What thoughts and emotions are you experiencing as you're reading this chapter? Are you feeling more organized and motivated? Are you fired up? Are you feeling more in tune with your goals? Can you see your destination more clearly? Are you finding these strategies possible? Document your feelings and thoughts around this page or in your journal.

Now is a good time to pause and take a few deep breaths. As you become clearer and more confident about your plans, I hope your internal protectors begin to cooperate with you in this journey and no longer sabotage your actions. If they've been in tune with your efforts, take a moment to thank them. If your inner critic has been a bit cynical, gently remind this part of you that you're working on getting better organized and creating a plan, taking action, and keeping track of your progress.

Now that you have learned how to get better organized and are ready to make things happen for yourself, it's time to move on to Sergio's Take. In this section, Sergio shares how these organizational strategies have taken his studio practice and business to the next level.

Sergio's Take

As you read from Dr. Yanina, I was not exactly organized when we first met. On the contrary, I was a "go with the flow and let's see what happens" kind of guy. Planning for the future was not exactly something I did. In my defense, I was in my twenties. That should count for something. Right? Perhaps I'm the creative type like you. My mind wants to create and be free. It does not like to get caught up in all this organization and productivity stuff. When it comes to my art studio, life can go on as long as I know where things are. It is only when I stop finding my tools and start wasting time that I have to clean up and organize my tools, paints, and brushes. My home studio is controlled chaos. For the record, Dr. Yanina does not have any jurisdiction there. My studio is off-limits to her wonderful desire to keep things neat around the house.

I'm disorganized and distracted. I have a hard time following up on long storybooks, movies, or stories. During a long conversation, I have to work hard to stay focused, or my mind begins to wander around. I also tend to procrastinate on the things I know will be boring to do. I have the bad habit of writing sticky notes with something that needs to be done, and because I wrote it, my mind thinks it's done. I often forget to look at my to-do lists or sticky notes in front of my face. Yes, that's me.

Now that you have a better idea of how my mind works in this area, be reassured there is hope for you as there was for me. Besides all the drawbacks listed above, I managed to get things done in my early years. Similar to the controlled chaos, I could get ahead and accomplish things. A few years after I got married to Dr. Yanina, I started to pursue my MFA. I was also working full-time at a marketing firm, and we had our first child. As you can imagine, life became complicated. I had no choice but to get serious about learning new organization skills, learn about productivity tools, and start new healthier habits. The responsibilities of family life had begun to set in. I quickly knew the way I got things done in the past was not going to hold on for too long.

I experienced a mindset shift and began to make better decisions on how I used my time. I got myself one of those digital Palm Pilots. Remember those? They were the electronic devices with the little pencil you could write on the screen; it was before smartphones. The Palm Pilot promised to be the solution to all my messy problems. I tried hard to get organized. I wrote down all my to-do's, made lists, and added reminders. Things would work out well for a while, but as it is in my nature, I would get bored and fail to keep up after a few months. I got tired of the little pencil. Trying to write was more complicated than the time I was hoping to save.

When it comes to organization tools such as the Palm Pilot, apps, notepads, computer programs, motivational videos, self-help podcasts, and hundreds of sticky notes, I have tried them all. I had to work hard at becoming organized and productive. Here is the good news. It is a conscious choice that one makes every day to get better at it. Over time, your effort accumulates into something good. You eventually can get to the other side and turn your kryptonite into your superpower. That is right; you can become more organized and productive without sacrificing happiness and enjoyment.

In a way, this journey of turning procrastination into action has allowed me to understand motivation, self-discipline, and how I occupy my time in and out of the studio. I was so focused on getting better at it that I may have turned into a productivity freak. My wife, Dr. Yanina, has to remind me constantly to slow down and take breaks. By no means is this healthy either. Busyness is equally as bad as procrastination and disorganization. The point I want to make is you can figure out a strategy that works best for you and stick with it.

When artists ask me how I manage my art career, curating, running a gallery, coaching, and being super active in social media, they usually follow up with comments like these: "You must be cloning yourself. There have to be Sergio clones running around doing things for you."

I laugh, of course, and tell them I wish it were true. I could use some of those clones. The reality is I learned time is a valuable asset that should not be wasted. I learned how to choose the tools I need to make life easier and organize my day without feeling guilty if something does not get done.

One of the top secrets of successful artists is understanding and remembering the big picture. You see, you can be very busy every day of your life and not make much progress. Busyness is not equal to effectiveness. Busyness is not the goal of this chapter. You may appear very busy, but you are in the same spot or very close to where you started. That is not the way we want to live our lives. We want to know the activities we choose to do will yield progress or reward. We want to be happy with our work and feel fulfilled, so we are excited to get up every morning and be the best artist we can be.

Without visualizing the big picture, you will have a hard time making substantial progress. Here is where many artists get stuck. We get caught up in the mundane everyday tasks of making posts on social media, answering emails, updating our websites, doing our marketing, and so on. All we want to do is get done with those tasks so we can run back to the studio and make art. Does this sound familiar?

We have this enormous pressure to have a website, social media, email newsletter, and everything else necessary to run a successful art career. We feel great things will come our way if we do all these things. In other words, get busy so you can succeed. Do not get me wrong. If you do not reply to that important email, perhaps you will lose a tremendous opportunity. But the question here is, how do all these tasks relate to the big picture? What are you trying to accomplish in six months, one year, or five years? It is time to look at the big picture, and visualize where you want to arrive.

Big picture thinking means setting real achievable goals, not only New Year's resolutions. It also means taking time to stop every so often to think and assess where you've been and where you believe you are going so you can make the necessary adjustments and refine your strategy. When Dr. Yanina and I decided to create *The Goal Setting and Progress System for Artists* course, we did it to help me. I needed this tool to keep my eye on the big picture. Otherwise, I get distracted and easily lose focus. Once we saw how much it helped me achieve my career goals, we decided to help others. We committed to making it a free resource and have been teaching it for a few years during *The Goal Setting Boot Camp for Artists*, a complimentary online event for artists. By now, thousands of artists have taken this boot camp and have become much better at making and accomplishing their art business goals.

In this boot camp, there is a session titled "When Your Goals Meet Your Daily Habits." It is one of my favorite lessons to teach. Everybody starts the year with great goals and expectations. Unless you introduce your goals to your daily habits, there will be a war inside of you. You see, your habits have seniority. They have been with you for a long time. They like things as they are. Good and bad habits have learned to coexist and live harmoniously. Your adopted habits hate every new year because they know you will bring new guests into their space, and those new guests are coming to make themselves at home. These newcomers are your New Year's resolutions, including goals for yourself and your art career.

What makes your old habits so uncomfortable is your new goals arrive happy, cheery, excited, and with an abundance of joy. They want to come in and change the furniture, open the windows, clean up the mess, and simply disrupt the status quo. Your new goals are like Chef Gordon Ramsey in his show *Kitchen Nightmares*. Your goals come to expose all the dirt and shortcuts your bad habits have created. Chef Ramsey is very good at that. I love that show! He makes it clear he is there to create, stir things up, and change the status quo. This immediately creates resistance among the restaurant staff.

Similarly, nothing will change in your life unless you introduce your new goals to your daily habits and mindfully understand changes will need to happen for you to achieve these goals. Otherwise, the status quo will quickly set in, and it will be another year you'll wish you had followed up on your goals. *Oh well, there is always the next year*, we tell ourselves.

I love the show *Kitchen Nightmares* because there is always a boiling point—that moment when the music stops and Chef Ramsey faces the kitchen staff. Everyone finally realizes things need to change, or the restaurant will close down for good. That is the breaking point when the kitchen staff starts working together and helping each other. They can finally see the big picture, not only their task in the kitchen. At the end of the show is the grand finale, when all the new customers walk through the doors to completely new decor, a new menu, and new ways of working. There is a big picture mentality, and it makes the whole difference.

That is precisely what happens when we get to the end of the year, look back at our art career, and tell ourselves, *I may not have achieved every single goal, but I made significant advancements in my art career.* That's all. It is the difference between frustration and fulfillment. It is about seeing the big picture. You may not get all you want in your art career, but you know when you have moved closer and closer to where you want to be.

This is what I have for you, my friend. Create smart and exciting goals for your art career. Do not get so caught up in the daily routine that you forget about the big picture. The exercise Dr. Yanina has prepared for you below is exactly what *The Goal Setting and Progress System for Artists* course is all about. It has the potential to change your life and the outcome of your art career. Take it seriously.

Diving Deeper

Let's get better organized and back on track! Keep in mind it's going to take some time if organization is something you've been struggling with for a while. It will also take intentionality, tons of reminders, and, if need be, an accountability partner to help you get things done. There's no shame in that!

1. Personal Growth Destination

    - What is the main goal you want to set for yourself?
      _____
      _____

    - Why is this goal important to you?
      _____
      _____

    - Identify one to three action steps needed to kick start the journey toward achieving this goal. Assign a deadline for each action step.
      _____
      _____

    - Write down the resources and tools you'll need to take your action steps.
      _____
      _____

2. Career or Business Destination

    - What is the main goal you want to set for your creative business?
      _____
      _____

    - Why is this goal necessary for your professional or business growth?
      _____
      _____

- Identify one to three action steps needed to kick start the journey toward achieving this goal. Assign a deadline for each action step.

  _____

  _____

- Write down the resources and tools you'll need to take your action steps.

  _____

  _____

3. Track Your Progress

   You'll be using the Monthly Goal Progress Tracking Chart that Sergio and I created for this exercise. You'll find it in the Appendix of the book. You are welcome to create your own form. Each week, you'll be asked to document your progress by placing an X mark and the week number in the tracking form. As the weeks go by, you want to see your mark move closer to the green dot, which indicates the task has been completed. We know that sooner or later, life will throw you a curveball. That's why we have the *rollover to the next month* option. If you did not complete an action step this month, simply roll it over and work on it next month. No shame or guilt allowed!

   - Print the Monthly Goal Progress Tracking Chart to begin tracking your progress.
   - Write down your main goal and indicate the month you're working on.
   - Write down one to three action steps you have identified to get you closer to achieving your main goal. Remember, let's focus on 1-3 at a time.

- At the end of each week, track your progress. Place an X on the line and write the numbers 1, 2, 3, or 4 under each mark. The number refers to the week you're documenting.
- Place the X and the number representing the week you're documenting in the area that accurately indicates how close you are to completing the action step. Repeat this step for each action step you've written in the form.
- As a reference, the circle refers to the starting point. The triangle indicates the task is halfway completed. Finally, the check mark indicates the task has been completed.

Each form documents one month at a time. Therefore, you must print a new form each month. If need be, roll over any incomplete action step to the next month until it is accomplished.

Wrapping It Up

I encourage you to remain optimistic so you can continue experiencing clarity and confidence to get the results you deserve for yourself. Remember, this is an ongoing process. Trust yourself! You'll get better at staying organized and motivated.

Before I let you go, let's take a moment to acknowledge the difficult and intense inner work you completed! I recommend you take some time to rest and decompress. Consider doing a guided meditation, breathing, or relaxation exercise to calm and clear your mind. A power nap also works wonders. You can also share your self-discoveries with your accountability partner or a trusted person. When you're ready, come back to Chapter Six, where we'll be focusing on boosting self-trust and self-motivation.

CHAPTER SIX
TRUSTING MYSELF ONCE AND FOR ALL

One of the things I love about facilitating emotional wellness workshops and retreats for creatives is the deep and honest conversations that happen following the sessions. The conversations usually tap into the challenges, insecurities, and fears often resulting from hustling in the creative world. Simply put, it's the psychological ups and downs of the creative's journey.

Again and again, artists share their passion for creativity and difficulties with getting their art out there. Some feel uncomfortable about sharing their art with others, especially with strangers. Most artists will tell you they would rather be in their studio making art instead of using their time on marketing and sales efforts. I often hear, "I signed up to be an artist, not a salesperson or marketer!"

It can be intimidating to share and talk about your art with others. It becomes more complicated when you are the one promoting and selling your work—because you don't have an art manager or someone who can sell your art. It can feel awkward and uncomfortable. After all, your art is a window to your life, values, thoughts, and even your soul.

Maybe you're thinking, Dr. Yanina, it's safer to share my work only with people I know. That way, I won't have to face criticism, and I'll have more emotional energy to create." If this is how you feel, how is this choice helping you grow, evolve, and succeed as an artist? Will this choice help you overcome your insecurities and develop a profitable art business? I have never met someone who has experienced personal and professional growth without experiencing growing pains and a dose of self-doubt and facing obstacles along the way. Growth takes place when we let go of our comfort zone and intentionally step into the intimidating growth zone.

If you ever doubt yourself, your art, or your abilities, you're not alone. It's normal to feel vulnerable when sharing, promoting, and selling an extension of yourself. Your art is a reflection of your values, beliefs, thoughts, and opinions and a peek into your inner world. You're proud of your creation and excited about sharing it with the world. Yet, the possibility of harsh criticism or insensitive feedback from others may be preventing you from pushing yourself beyond limits and achieving success. No wonder selling your work can test your confidence and self-trust.

As a contemporary creative person, you have to promote yourself and your art if you want to sell. Yet, a sense of overwhelm and frustration emerges from this reality. Consequently, many artists experience self-doubt and even second-guess the quality of their work. *How will others perceive me? Is my art good enough? What if I post my art on social media and end up getting hate comments? Whom am I kidding? My art will never be like the art of (insert name of the artist you admire)."*

Social media marketing and online sales are becoming essential tools for a profitable art business. The aftermath of the global coronavirus pandemic has made this situation unavoidable for those wanting to increase exposure and sales. In the past, when galleries represented an artist, they took care of the marketing, sales, and other managerial responsibilities. Although the latter may still be the case for some artists, most artists face the reality that if they don't promote their work, especially online, sales won't happen. Another truth is how the pandemic has also impacted and changed how art galleries conduct their business. As we know, some did not survive this impact, whereas others rely primarily on online sales. This situation has also challenged artists to become entrepreneurial and intentional about making themselves known in this competitive industry. No wonder self-trust is put to the test!

If you're asking yourself what you can do to trust yourself and your art to overcome these challenges and succeed in your art career, this chapter is for you. Here, I'm sharing three mindset shift strategies to increase self-trust, be bold, and make decisions that will advance your art career. As a reminder, mindset is adopted attitudes and thinking patterns that shape how we make sense of ourselves and the world around us. We can choose to keep or unlearn them.

The first mindset shift strategy ton increase self-trust is to crush your impostor beliefs. At least 82% of people face feelings of impostor phenomenon.[1] That is more evident among high achievers. Impostor phenomenon is the tendency to doubt and minimize your abilities, talents, and accomplishments. You believe you're fooling others into thinking you are someone you are not. You may also have a fear of being exposed as a fraud or having your secret discovered. You struggle with owning your achievements and may experience a sense of unworthiness that doesn't align with what others think about you. If I describe how you've been feeling as an artist, it's no surprise stress, anxiety, and perhaps symptoms of depression may affect the quality of your life. Maybe you're avoiding taking risks which, you know, is essential in growing your business or developing your career. Perhaps there's an inner voice telling you're not a real artist because you have to rely on a day job right now.

In some people, these impostor beliefs can result from the competitive culture that glorifies winners, shames poor performance, and expects us to give more while caring less about ourselves. The focus is on achieving results not on investing in relationships. Other times, these beliefs are either self-induced or based on labels imposed by others. Some examples of these labels are:

- I'm a loser.
- I'm not a real artist.
- I don't have what it takes to succeed.
- I'm invisible.
- I've always been a loser.
- I can't do anything right.

We know labels can impact the way we view ourselves. Some have been carrying past wounds resulting from hurtful words or labels given by family members and people in their past or current relationships. Maybe you were told at a young age that you are not loved or aren't good enough. Maybe someone said you lack what it takes to succeed in this world or told you that you'll always be a starving artist. Labels imposed by others can only work if you choose to welcome them. We can allow our insecurities and self-doubt to convince ourselves to stop trying and internalize the labels imposed on us by others. Alternatively, we can train our minds to adopt an optimistic attitude and reject the hurtful labels imposed on us. You have the choice and the ability to internalize or reject them. My invitation to you is to reject and unlearn these hurtful thoughts. List these labels, label them as toxic, and intentionally reject them. Add this exercise to your emotional cleansing efforts. It will give you peace of mind and a sense of ownership. We'll dedicate some time to this issue in the *Diving Deep*er section below.

Not all reactions to the impostor phenomenon are harmful. To some individuals, these thoughts spark a desire for self-growth. They get motivated to improve themselves when they believe others judge or make false assumptions about them. They take it as a challenge and choose to invest in self-growth. A level of self-doubt inspires them to become their best version. They want to prove to themselves, and perhaps others, that they're capable of reaching a specific goal. For instance, if a colleague was accepted in a prestigious art exhibition, they believe they can have the same opportunity by pushing themselves and putting their mind and resources into it. It's not about feeling entitled or jealous. It's about being inspired by other people's successes, challenging themselves to achieve higher standards, and thriving. It would be ideal if all of us would react to our impostor beliefs this way. Wouldn't it be wonderful if all creatives reacted this way to their impostor feelings?

A more common reaction to the impostor phenomenon is allowing these thoughts to slow down our self-growth and feed our insecurities. In other words, we begin to minimize our capabilities, come up with excuses to justify a lack of results, or simply give up. It gets complicated when we start to play the dangerous comparison game. We begin to believe we don't have what it takes to succeed because we're not like someone else. This game is so destructive it can potentially end your creative career if you aren't careful.

Frankly, it is almost impossible to stop comparing yourself to others and to commit to never doing it again. It's human nature. As I've mentioned before, a healthy dose of comparison can spark a desire to thrive. It's not healthy when we make it a habit to be peeking into other people's lives constantly only to end up feeling envious and miserable. The more you compare yourself to others, the more you deprive yourself of investing in your success. My challenge to you is this. What if you do less peer comparison and start focusing on living fully? What will your mental state and quality of life look like if you take this stance?

There is one way to use comparison to improve and reach excellence. In the next mindset shift strategy, I share how this type of comparison can lead to self-growth and boost your confidence. Before we get to that strategy, let's finish with the nutty impostor beliefs.

The more I speak with artists, the more I am convinced the impostor phenomenon is not a stranger to creatives. Of course, artists aren't the only ones facing this challenge. Other professionals also fall into this trap. Anyone who wants to improve and grow can potentially experience these thoughts. I am not immune to the impostor phenomenon either. I remember experiencing these feelings intensively when I began my career as a psychologist and a few times later on in my life.

I'm sure you agree one of the most common triggers for creatives is marketing and selling their artwork because this involves vulnerability and savviness. Many artists who are not in tune with technology and social media may feel inadequate and uncomfortable about sharing their lives on the internet. Others simply feel intimidated about sharing their art because they fear others may question their work, judge their credentials, or make hurtful assumptions.

Since impostor beliefs or thoughts are one of the most common issues bringing creatives down, let's do something about it and change things for the better. Here are five tips to help you overcome these feelings and continue your journey toward trusting yourself once and for all.

The first tip is to recognize and acknowledge that no one knows your artwork as well as you do. The key here is to understand you are the expert on your art. Don't waste a minute or ounce of your energy on thinking you're going to make a mistake when you're sharing your why or the story behind your art with a prospective client. Seriously! Some artists have a hard time absorbing this truth. They're scared they'll mess up or make a fool of themselves when they talk about their art. How can you make a mistake when you're talking about your creation? It's impossible!

This leads me to tip number two: allow yourself to be the expert. In reality, whatever you say about your art, people will believe you as long as you're authentic and truthful. People love to hear the stories behind your art and why your art matters. Artist talks are an amazing opportunity to engage the people in the room with your art and to connect with you. Many people buy art because they connect with it intellectually or emotionally. How can people question you about your artwork when they don't have the grounds to do so? It's okay to talk about your art! There is nothing to be afraid of as long as you can verbalize your story in a way that makes sense. This leads me to my next tip.

Tip number three is to prepare yourself so t your story flows. When you're prepared, you feel confident about yourself. To some artists, talking about their artwork may come naturally. They can talk about their work for hours. Many artists may need to prepare beforehand, and that's fine. They may have to work on their personal story and the narrative of their art. They may even practice in front of the mirror or with a friend. If you're one of the artists in need of some practice, take the time to prepare yourself. As Sergio would suggest, take time to reflect on your story, influences, and values. Once you reflect on these areas, take time to write your narrative. Have available a brief version of the story behind your artwork. We refer to this version as your elevator pitch. The more you take the time to reflect on your work, your why, and why others should care about it, the more your message will flow. Consequently, you'll persuade others to connect and purchase it.

Now, you're ready for tip number four. Do your reality check. When impostor thoughts invade your mind, follow the same strategies I've shared with you in Chapter Three. Remember the impostor phenomenon is a form of mindset blocks and negative thinking patterns. Ask yourself these questions: *Are these thoughts facts? What evidence do I have to prove my negative thoughts wrong?*

Identify the circumstances fueling this thought. These are the triggers you need to avoid. Write down the facts you have to prove you can accomplish the goal you set for yourself. Next, write down what others have been affirming about you and your work. If you have no evidence to support such thoughts, they might not be accurate. This is when you also use the formula I taught you in Chapter Four to crush negative thinking and actively bring yourself back to rational thought:

STOP + LABEL + TOSS + REPLACE = HEALTHIER THINKING

My last tip to crushing impostor beliefs or thoughts is to make a habit of celebrating your successes. Whether you label your success as small or large is irrelevant. Any success is important and contributes to your growth. None of us are born walking, talking, and making decisions for ourselves. It's a developmental process that takes a long time and involves a series of mistakes and taking baby steps. Ask any parent how wonderful it feels to witness their child experience a developmental stage regardless of how big or small.

If you catching yourself brushing off your successes constantly or not even noticing them, it's time to commit to paying more attention and celebrating it. For instance, if someone says you're a very talented artist, and your first reaction is to justify their statement, try this. Do not respond to this compliment right away. If you do, you'll likely provide a response that will demean yourself or diminish your ability. Stop, take a deep breath, and aim to say something positive: *Thank you! I appreciate your words.*

That's it! Avoid saying things like, *the stars aligned in my favor, it was mere luck, a fluke, or a lucky break.* There's no need to justify your abilities, experiences, and potential. Embrace each of them with gratitude.

If this is an area you're struggling with, I recommend documenting in your wellness journal encounters with people who share a sincere compliment or acknowledge your efforts. Take a screenshot or print it if someone sends you a text, direct message on social media, or an email complimenting your art or your hard work,. Staple it in your wellness journal. I always say we should never rely solely on other people's feedback for motivation. Yet, I don't underestimate the power of these reminders either. It feels great when people acknowledge your hard work and give you the credit you well deserve.

It's essential you learn and practice self-motivation strategies to keep going even in the face of setbacks and obstacles. A powerful practice is personal affirmations. If you've never heard of personal affirmations, don't worry. I'll be teaching you the value of this self-motivation strategy and how to write your own in the next chapter.

To recap, the more you document external feedback and practice self-motivation and gratitude, the stronger your confidence will become and the more you'll trust yourself. Yes, you can overcome impostor thoughts and beliefs. I can't promise similar thoughts will never emerge again; they can be quite sneaky. You have learned tools to fight back and no longer allow them to define who you are. My question to you is, how will you react to the impostor beliefs lingering in your head? Will you let them ignite or slow down your self-growth?

The second mindset shift strategy to help you increase self-trust and experience personal growth is to compare yourself to yourself. I love teaching this strategy to creatives and anyone who wants to live a happier and more fulfilling life. It's a simple yet very powerful strategy. The truth is, we've been comparing ourselves to others since we were little people. Your first-grade classmate always seemed to bring better snacks to a school than you. Perhaps your neighbor's kids always got the coolest toys for Christmas. Maybe your best friend always seemed to date the hottest boys in high school when you didn't even have a date for your high school prom. Unfortunately, this tendency doesn't go away when we grow up. How many times do you find yourself scrolling down social media posts and comparing yourself to other fellow artists? I venture to say, every day. You may think to yourself, *we all do it*! Have you paid attention to the emotions that emerge when you compare yourself to others?

Allow me to share a scenario with you. It's the start of a new day full of possibilities and opportunities. You find yourself on social media scrolling post after post from friends, family members, and fellow artists instead of setting yourself up for success from the get-go. You spend minutes or even hours on social media scrolling and reading about other artists' successes. You get stuck on the posts of fellow artists who seem to be doing better than you are. You can't help but wonder why those artists are doing so well, and you're not. *Why is Sergio getting these amazing opportunities for his art career? Why do I never hear about them? Why does he seem to get into these solo exhibitions in museums and I haven't been able to do so? What does he have that I don't? I make good art too*!

That is how the comparison game starts destroying your confidence and self-trust. It happens when we compare ourselves to others not because we admire or feel inspired by them but because we envy them. It's our nature to compare ourselves to others, especially when they have already arrived at the destination you've wanted to reach for so long. The vicious social media makes it so easy to get caught up in the comparison game. It's so easy to waste valuable time scrolling for hours. we don't even notice how much time we're wasting, which makes matters worse.

When we get caught up in the dangerous comparison game, we end up experiencing inadequacy and self-doubt and may even question our purpose. We wonder why these artists are evolving and we're not. I can tell you one reason why they're succeeding in their art career. They are probably not wasting valuable time scrolling on social media comparing themselves to other artists. They're using their time wisely and investing in their growth instead of getting caught up in the comparison game or senseless scrolling.

Why do we have an urge to compare ourselves to others? Some people compare themselves because they want to justify their envy or lack of effort. Others use comparison to mask inner conflicts and justify insecurities hurting them. Each person has reasons to compare themselves to others or desire what others want. I've learned that unless we use comparison for inspiration, there's no beneficial outcome at all. The end road will always lead to toxicity and unhappiness.

Unless you're looking for inspiration, there's no reason to compare yourself to others because you are unique, and you matter. It's like comparing chicken and oranges. Although they share the same purpose, which is to nurture our bodies, they belong to different food groups (*i.e.*, protein and fruits). Each has its own unique texture, taste, and nutritional benefits. If your body needs fiber, vitamin C, and folate, the chicken won't meet that need. Oranges contain very little protein and fat. Therefore, it wouldn't make sense to compare them even when both are healthy foods.

This is true for us too. It wouldn't make sense for me to compare myself to you or for you to compare yourself to Sergio. Each of us has different lifestyles, opportunities, connections, relationships, and unique talents. It makes self-worth contingent on achievement. Self-worth involves so much more! Our society glorifies competition. A level of competition can inspire innovation and a desire to improve. When toxicity gets in the mix, it becomes an unhealthy way of living. Understand it's unrealistic and unfair to you to compare yourself to others. You are so much more!

There's only one way comparisons can lead to self-growth and fulfilling life. It is possible when you choose only to compare yourself to you. It makes more sense to compare your past self to the person you are today. Then, months from now, compare yourself to who you are at that time in your life. In other words, you compare your past self to your present self to identify growth or a lack thereof. In the *Diving Deeper* section below, you'll have the opportunity to document your past self and today's self so you can compare both versions. You will also compare these two versions of yourself with your future self when the time comes. It will make sense once you complete the self-comparison exercise.

Regardless of whether you see it as small or large, comparing your progress leads to greater confidence and self-satisfaction. It also leads to self-awareness as you identify the areas that need attention and improvement. On the contrary, comparing yourself to others leads to self-doubt, lack of confidence, and defeat.

On a side note, keep in mind we face plateau stages in our life. This is normal. We hit a plateau for many reasons. One is when we face circumstances beyond our control or unexpected. An example of hitting a plateau stage is waiting on an art residency committee to approve your application or lacking ideas as you begin a new series of work. As you begin to practice the self-comparison method, you may discover your growth has been minimal or non-existent. It can be due to circumstances out of your control or poor choices you've made. See your situation as motivation to improve rather than labeling it as a hopeless failure. Don't get stuck on your growth not being where you want it to be at this moment. Remember, you have the opportunity to keep moving forward for as long as there's one day after another.

Regarding circumstances that are out of our control or slow down our growth, let's talk about the year 2020. I'm sure you're rolling your eyes or even frowning as soon as you read that. As you recall, we were hit with the global coronavirus pandemic. The world as we knew it stopped. Lockdowns were in place, and people were not allowed to congregate. Some businesses closed temporarily, and others closed permanently. The art world experienced a freeze, and many galleries had to reinvent the way they do business. Many moved their business online, whereas others fought hard to stay afloat. For most of us, experiencing a global pandemic was new and unknown. We didn't know what to expect and how to go about life under these circumstances. The rise of mental health issues was too steep and concerning. Many people stayed home and did not leave their houses for months. Some people had company; others were all alone. Some lost loved ones to the virus, and others experienced severe physical consequences. As you know, social events were forbidden, grocery shopping was mainly done online and delivered, and in-person human connections were almost non-existent.

During this time, creatives lacked opportunities to perform, exhibit, or share their creativity with others. I spoke to many artists who expressed their fears, worries, frustration, and sadness due to the unexpected lockdowns. Most in-person art events were canceled. Maybe opportunities and exhibitions you had lined up for 2020 and 2021 were also canceled or postponed. There's no doubt the coronavirus pandemic has taken a toll on our physical and mental health.

As we continue to recover from its aftermath, we can't ignore the consequences we're experiencing. One of them is a lack of or minimal self-growth. Maybe you experienced minimal to no self-growth as you compare your past self to today's self. Perhaps the growth has been significant. If the former is hitting home, don't feel discouraged. Don't linger on this thought or get angry with yourself for a past you cannot change. I invite you instead to use your energy and time wisely. Today, do something about it. Take action, and create the change you want to see in your life! Set new goals, and work on a plan of action. Identify which areas in your life are thirsty for growth. My dear reader, we cannot change the past. We can't minimize or ignore it either. We can, however, redefine our present and take action toward living a better future.

As you begin to adopt the self-comparison method, I invite you to ask yourself these questions: What do I want to accomplish now? Which area in my life needs to be nurtured or changed? Where do I see myself, my art, and business twelve, eighteen, or twenty-four months from today? Action leads to confidence! Trust your art and stay focused on your progress.

If you don't believe in your art, no one will! If you're having second thoughts about your art, try this. Even when you don't believe in yourself or your art yet, don't be afraid to take risks. Tell yourself every day you matter and your art matters. Remind yourself why you make the art you do and why it matters. As you take action and begin to see results, your confidence will improve naturally. The key is to prepare yourself and never go blindfolded. Remember what I mentioned earlier in this chapter. Whether you're applying for a residency, writing a proposal, or marketing your art in social media, always prepare yourself. Take time to create a plan of action to achieve your goal. Do your research, work hard, and keep fine-tuning your skills.

Start with curiosity, and take the necessary steps to convert your interest into an opportunity. I can't stress enough that the more you prepare yourself, the more confidence you will feel about yourself and the decisions you make about your art practice. Self-trust and confidence are the results of proving yourself you can do it. As you document your progress through the self-comparison method, you'll begin to see your progress and adjust as you go.

You have your energy, experiences, and opportunities. They are all valid. Take some time to acknowledge and embrace each of them. Focus on your growth and inner self so you can give back to others through your actions and your art. Don't get distracted by what others are doing. My invitation to you is to compare less so you can live more. The less you compare yourself to others, the more you can focus on your growth and the healthier your state of mind will be. Use this short mantra to remind yourself about this powerful truth: Compare less, live more.

> The less you compare yourself to others, the more you can focus on your growth and the healthier your state of mind will be.

My last mindset strategy to increase self-trust is to be a lifelong learner. It's important you invest in knowledge and never stop learning. Find opportunities to educate yourself about the areas that will help you evolve as a person and an artist. The art world is constantly evolving. Art sales strategies and marketing are constantly changing. I encourage you to learn as much as you can about the business of art.

Pursue professional development opportunities and find support.

Permit yourself to ask for help. There's no shame or guilt in asking for help. Everyone needs it at some point. One of the best decisions you can make for yourself is to put your pride or reservations aside and seek help so you can succeed. Find a trusted and knowledgeable coach to guide you in your art career. Professional support groups can also help build up confidence and authentic relationships. You can learn from other people's experiences and perspectives. You might find out your perspective needs some tweaking, or you might realize you're heading in the right direction to create a sustainable art career. Sergio and I believe so much in lifelong learning and the value of belonging to an authentic professional support group that we founded the Art NXT Level Academy to address these needs. I can't stress enough the importance of becoming a lifelong learner and surrounding yourself with authentic fellow creatives. Knowledge combined with action can turn your world around in a powerful way.

Now, it's time to check out Sergio's Take as he shares about his journey toward building and maintaining self-trust amid adversities. He also shares his take on how the self-comparison method has been pivotal in his professional growth. Remember, reaching confidence and trusting yourself is a lifelong process. Be patient and exercise self-compassion.

> **Remember, reaching confidence and trusting yourself is a lifelong process.**

Sergio's Take

Trusting in yourself is easier said than done. Sometimes we believe we fully trust in ourselves only to find out that often we face doubts and insecurities when we least expect it. Ironically, when I am writing the response to this chapter, I am going through a week of self-doubt. I don't remember experiencing this second-guessing attitude in a long time regarding my art career. Like you, I have small moments of doubt in the studio. *Will I ruin my work if I use red or blue? Will I lose followers if I post this photo on Instagram?*

Those are normal doubts that happen in our heads as we make choices daily. Those come with the territory of being an artist. The problem is when doubt or lack of trust prevents us from moving ahead or dilutes our focus.

I'm neither a cavalier decision-maker nor an over-calculating individual. I am somewhere in between. I know what I want. I look at the options, take enough time to analyze my current situation, weigh potential risks and gains to make a choice, and move on. That's it. Life involves an endless selection of choices. I typically don't look back and ponder what would happen if I had taken the blue pill instead of the red pill like in the movie *The Matrix*. I accept the fact I made a decision and move on.

This week, I have been experiencing a rollercoaster in my mind. Let me explain how I got here. In the Fall of 2021, I got interested in NFTs. I spent an ungodly number of hours learning, investigating, talking to others, and listening to everything related to NFTs. From cryptocurrencies, blockchain, generative art to DAOs, it has been a learning curve. If you have no idea what those terms mean, I get it. Only six months ago, I had no clue either. I had heard so much about it in the news and art magazines that it caught my interest. When I turned fifty last year, I thought it would be a good challenge to learn something new, something that would be interesting, useful, and challenging. I decided to immerse myself and learn all about NFTs.

Fast forward three months into that decision, and I am a few days away from minting and releasing my first NFT collection to the public. You would think releasing a collection online would be no big deal after more than fifty solo shows, and 150 group shows in over ten countries. Other than learning the technical aspects of NFT's and how to do it, it should be easy. What's the big deal, right? Yet, as of this morning, I have been losing sleep trying to figure out if the art collection I created for the NFTs is the right one. After all, this is a whole new space and very different from what I know in the art world. The rules, the collectors, and the way you sell and get paid is different. Everything new.

Here is my dilemma, I have many art series to start with and many ideas on what to do. A few weeks ago, I selected one of them. I have spent a lot of time digitizing and editing the art in this collection. I've been looking at what others are doing in the NFT marketplaces, and I thought to myself, *Is my work out of place? Will this fit as an NFT? Should I have started with my newest work instead of this older series? Should I have created a new art on my iPad like many other artists are doing? Is this series good enough for NFT? Will collectors like it? After all, they seem to be a lot younger than those in the traditional art world.*

Before I knew it, I found myself second-guessing my choices left and right. What on earth? A choice is a choice, and I move on. That is how I've always rolled. Well, not this time. The truth is after I read this chapter Dr. Yanina so eloquently wrote, I had to reground myself and apply her teachings. I had to acknowledge this doubt is hindering me from moving forward and feeling confident about my collection. I had to compare myself to myself and stop comparing to others who are different artists than me. I had to recognize those thoughts of insecurity and apply the **STOP + LABEL + TOSS + REPLACE** strategy to move on.

Oh my goodness! I couldn't believe I was getting caught up in the self-doubt trap. After all, I am the confident artist who can take the cell phone at any given moment and do an Instagram live about marketing, social media, or interview someone on the spot. Why would I have these huge self-doubts about something I have created before? I believe the answer is because it is something new, and I have never experienced something like this before in my career. I sincerely tell you I have not been this undecided about my art in a long time.

Let's take a quick look at how it all started. All I wanted to do was push myself into a new adventure. I wanted to challenge myself and grow as an artist. That's it. It was supposed to be good and exciting. That is, until I got to this point of being on verge of releasing my project to the eyes of the world. The thoughts of doubt held me captive. I don't know what you may be going through right now. I'm sure you had experiences like these before where you are about to deliver the work to a gallery waiting for you, or you are about to send that email with samples of your art to a curator or perhaps a meeting you will have with a potential client. All of a sudden, you have an intense moment of self-doubt. What we create is important to us. It has our sweat and tears written all over it, and rejection is a real thing. We want to avoid it at all costs.

Perhaps everything is going well for you right now, and you find yourself on a good streak of good fortune. Opportunities are coming in, and you feel good and proud of what is coming out of your art studio. That is awesome! Be aware that when doubt comes—and it will—you now have a plan to get out of it. Every hero has a villain. Maybe for you, doubt is the villain that continues to find a way to make you feel miserable, frustrated, or even paralyzed. Acknowledge your truth and take action.

Dr. Yanina has put together a wonderful set of questions and exercises below for you to dive in deeper and start trusting yourself once and for all. Once this chapter is written, I promise I will invite Dr. Yanina for coffee on your behalf for helping you and me trust ourselves when we need it the most. I feel ready to get my new collection out into the world! I hope you feel ready too! See you in the next chapter.

Diving Deeper

1. Crush your impostor beliefs. Who's the expert?

    - What's your impostor belief?
      _____
      _____

    - What is it based on?
      _____
      _____

        - Competitive culture
        - Self-induced beliefs
        - Labels imposed by others

    - It's easy to let impostor feelings and thoughts distract you from what truly matters. Let's take the time to break down this belief. Ask yourself:

        - Is this impostor belief a fact or an opinion?
          _____
          _____

        - What evidence do I have to prove my impostor belief wrong?
          _____
          _____

- What have other people been affirming about me and my work?

  _____

  _____

If you have no evidence to support such thoughts, they might not be accurate. This is when you also use my formula to crush negative thinking:

STOP + LABEL + TOSS + REPLACE = HEALTHIER THINKING

- Celebrate your wins!

  - Write down two recent small wins.

    _____

    _____

  - Write down two recent big wins.

    _____

    _____

  - How are you going to show gratitude and celebrate these wins?

    _____

    _____

Remember, you are the expert in your art! No one knows your artwork as well as or better than you do.

2. Reject toxic labels and replace them with healthier beliefs.

    Let's take some time to address the harmful labels keeping you from evolving into your better self. You've learned that labels imposed by others can only work if you choose to believe them. In this exercise, you'll learn to reject and unlearn these toxic labels.

    Write down below the labels hurting you right now. Next, identify the source of the label. Some examples are people from your childhood (*e.g.*, teachers, peers, neighbors, coworkers), family members, people in power (*e.g.*, formal or current boss), or yourself. These sources are your triggers. It's important to identify your triggers so you can avoid them as much as possible.

Toxic Label	Trigger
_____	_____
_____	_____

    Let's unlearn this toxic belief. For each label you wrote above, I invite you to write down the following sentences:

    - I will no longer allow the label of _____ define who I am." (Unlearn Belief)
    - From now on, _____. (Replacement Belief)

    Repeat these sentences every day until you replace the toxic belief with this new belief. We'll continue working on this exercise in the next chapter.

3. Compare Yourself to You

   Two Steps for Healthy Comparisons

   Step 1. Compare where you were yesterday to where you are today.

   Step 2. Compare where you are now to where you want to be tomorrow.

   You've learned that comparing yourself to yourself leads to a healthier perception of who you truly are and increases self-trust. You, too, can adopt this way of thinking! We're going to dive into the self-comparison method. You're welcome to use this book or your wellness journal to work on this healing exercise.

   - Write down a paragraph describing where you were yesterday (e.g., 6-months to 1-year ago).

     _____
     _____
     _____

   - Write down a paragraph describing where you are today.

     _____
     _____
     _____

   - List the areas where you've shown improvement or growth.

     _____
     _____
     _____

- List the areas where you've shown minimal to no growth. Should you be paying more attention to these areas or letting them go?

  _____
  _____
  _____

- Write down a paragraph describing where you want to be in the near future (*e.g.*, six or twelve months from today).

  _____
  _____
  _____

4. Let's take action!

   - What are the steps you'll be taking to become your tomorrow self? Alternatively, what are the steps you'll be taking to arrive at the place you want to be in the future?

     _____
     _____

   - Identify the habits that need to be let go of to become your tomorrow self.

     _____
     _____

   - Identify the habits or skills that need to be learned or polished to become your tomorrow self.

     _____
     _____

Allow yourself to go a little deeper.

- Whom do you tend to compare yourself with _____ (write down the name of the person you tend to compare yourself with)?
  _____
  _____

- Why are you comparing yourself to this person?
  _____
  _____

- What are you accomplishing by comparing yourself to this person?
  _____
  _____

- How is it working for you?
  _____
  _____

Are you ready to stop comparing yourself to this person and focus your energy on your growth? If so, commit to this change!

Today, commit yourself to replacing your comparison game with the self-comparison method: "I _____, commit to no longer compare myself to _____ because_____."

Wrapping It Up

Congratulations on completing Chapter Six! I commend you for your commitment to unlearn unhealthy habits and replace them with a healthy mindset that leads to self-trust. Give yourself the space to process the work you've completed in this chapter.

Schedule time to meet with your accountability partner. Share your takeaways and the steps you'll be taking to become your tomorrow self or arrive at the place you want to be in the near future. When you're ready, let's continue the journey in Chapter Seven, where you'll be exploring the healing benefits of personal affirmation.

CHAPTER SEVEN
REWIRING MY MIND THROUGH PERSONAL AFFIRMATIONS

Every day, we have the opportunity to wake up to possibilities and new experiences and do greater things. For as long as there's air passing through our lungs, we have a chance to change our future. We ought to focus on the things that matter most, but it's so difficult! We are constantly bombarded with ongoing distractions, and negativity always seems to make an entrance when we least expect it. We can't seem to escape these menaces. As soon as we open our social media accounts or watch the news, we find posts from others or antagonistic headlines that trigger our anger or insecurities and distract us from focusing on our progress. We even question ourselves and our abilities: *Why did I choose the creative path? Do I have what it takes to succeed in this highly competitive world? Why should I keep trying?*

As you keep working toward achieving your goals, don't be surprised if, some days, you wake up feeling fired up and ready to conquer the world, whereas other days, you can barely get up let alone feel motivated. Many of us experience these feelings more often than we want to. We all long for sunny days in our lives. That is why it is so important to learn ways to stay motivated and focus on your development regardless of distractions. We are human beings, and to err is human. You and I can be persistent, bounce back from setbacks, embrace grit, and keep moving forward!

In the previous chapter, I mentioned we need motivation and self-trust to get things done. Without motivation, we end up feeling stuck, frustrated, and paralyzed. Most of us rely so much on people's feedback for motivation. As I said before, I don't underestimate the power of people's words. It certainly feels good when others cheer you on, acknowledge, and support your efforts. Yet, we cannot only rely on others to make things happen for us and keep our motivation alive. It's an unrealistic expectation. People have busy lives. As much as they want to help us and be there for us, sometimes it's not possible. We've got to become self-sufficient and learn strategies to drive ourselves to take the initiative—even during those cloudy days.

I'm sure you've read about self-motivation strategies. It's as simple as typing "self-motivation strategies" in the internet search bar, and you'll get tons of links leading to articles, self-help books, courses, or online content. Some may be life-changing, whereas others might not work for you. We all have our definition of motivation, which is why not all strategies fit everybody.

The strategy I'm about to share with you is simple, yet it has proven practical and effective. I've been using this strategy for a while. I've also been teaching thousands of creatives through the Art NXT Level Academy, workshops, retreats, and social media content. Again and again, creatives have shared with me how this simple strategy has made a huge impact on the way they think. It has helped so many people become self-sufficient and connected with themselves at a deeper level. Others experience clarity, focus, motivation, and increased self-trust as they can visualize how they want their life to be. Let me clarify that merely because I say it's simple doesn't mean we're skipping deep inner work. It is happening!

A healthy way to stay motivated and achieve your goals is by writing your very own personal affirmation. It's your on-demand self-motivation strategy! One of the many purposes of this strategy is to train your brain to believe you already are the person you want to become or that you've already arrived at the place you want to reach. Another purpose is to keep you focused and grounded by reminding yourself about your whys, aspirations, new way of thinking, inner fuel, and the changes you want to see in yourself. Through this affirmation, you power up by telling yourself every day that you and the goals you have chosen truly matter, your accomplishments are important, and the life you want for yourself is possible. It is done through repetition and consistency. It's your daily adrenaline rush!

Personal affirmations rewire your mind intentionally. The more you remind yourself about your why, purpose, and intentions, the more you're training your mind to work on this new way of thinking instantly. These powerful truths will empower you to take action toward building the life you want. In the next few paragraphs, I will walk you through each step to write your affirmation. It will help you stay motivated, fired up, and want to do more.

> **The more you remind yourself about your why, purpose, and intentions, the more you're training your mind to work on this new way of thinking instantly.**

The first step to writing your personal affirmation is self-reflection. It's important to prepare yourself before you start to write. Let me share four essential preparation tips to ensure your personal affirmation is truthful and unique. My first tip is to set up a pleasant environment to work on this. You are welcome to prepare a warm cup of tea or coffee or serve yourself a glass of wine. Maybe you want to play your favorite playlist as background music to help you stay focused. Another suggestion is to light those scented candles, or open the windows and let fresh air flow through! Do whatever makes you feel comfortable, safe, and focused.

My second tip is to always write your personal affirmation in the present tense. This is very important because I want you to focus on the now and start thinking about being intentional and present. As you write your sentences in the present tense, you're instructing your mind to act on it right away. You invite your consciousness to start working on the action steps today and unlearn unhealthy thinking patterns by replacing them with your new way of thinking. If you use future tense (*e.g.*, I will), you're giving procrastination the green light. Your brain will read it as a non-urgent matter. Therefore, there's no need to take action right now. There's a difference between *I am no longer allowing fear to rule my life* and *I will work on defeating fear later*.

If you use past tense, you focus on what you cannot change. Since you cannot change the past, your mind may fall into the "Why should I bother?" trap. When you use the present tense, you're sending the messages to your brain that something can be done, and you need to take care of this matter now. Understanding the correct use of verb tense makes a powerful difference.

My third tip is to focus your affirmation on what you want to see happening in your life, not on what you're trying to eliminate from it. Including a list of all your fears, insecurities, and doubts in your affirmation is unhealthy and, honestly, useless. You're instead reminding yourself you no longer allow toxic beliefs and unpleasant circumstances to control your life.

My final tip is to ensure your affirmation reflects your new way of thinking and a new view of yourself. You're not the same person you were a year ago. You've changed and evolved. You are ready and determined to move your creative business or art career forward. You're no longer satisfied with your past self. You're ready for more! Make sure your affirmation reflects the new you.

As I walk you through the steps to write your very own personal affirmation, you're welcome to use the *Diving Deeper* section below to write each section, or use your wellness journal. If you keep up with me, you'll have your personal affirmation once you finish reading this chapter. If you're ready, let's go over the four steps to writing your personal affirmation. You can also refer to it as your mantra or declaration. Use the term that speaks to you best. In this chapter, I'm using "personal affirmation."

Now, you're ready for step two, which is the self-affirmation part of your personal affirmation. In this step, you begin by painting a clear picture in your head of who you are and what you want to accomplish. Here, you are affirming your value as an individual and commitment to this new way of thinking.

Next, focus your attention on identifying your inner fuel. What fires you up, excites you, and helps you stay focused? Identify your source of life or what pours out light from your soul. Take time to write down your current successes or wins (small or large) and what is going well for you right now. Avoid belittling or underestimating your wins. Maybe you recently finished a painting. Or you came up with an idea for a new series. Perhaps your latest artwork was accepted in a local art exhibition. Each of these is an example of a win.

Write down your positive attributes, what you value the most, and what gets you going. As I've previously mentioned, it's easier for our minds to remember negativity than positivity. That is why we have to reset our brains to focus on our inner beauty. Self-affirmation helps you embrace it. Once you have your answers, let's convert them into sentences. Now you have your self-affirmation paragraph.

Let me share an example of how a self-affirmation paragraph may look.

I am a gifted creative person, full of energy, love, and compassion toward others. I have a talent I consider to be a blessing for me and those around me. I'm passionate about sharing my creativity with others. I love how, through my art, I have the opportunity to make a difference in the lives of others. I believe in dignity, respect, and compassion for others. Being able to share my values and beliefs with others fills my heart. My source of light comes from my connection with my Creator and the presence of those who truly matter to me.

Let's move on to step three. In this step, you'll be writing your inner-affirmation. Here, we're going to name the emotions holding you back and highlight those that will help you thrive. I want you to think about the main areas in your life dragging you down. I've mentioned before we're focusing on what you want to see happening in your life, not on what you're trying to eliminate from it. To do that, we have to name our struggles first.

I can't encourage you enough to be truthful and honest with yourself as you work on your affirmation. Keep in mind you're the only one who will have access to it unless you choose to share it with others. If so, make sure you only share it with people you trust.

As you're working on this area, I invite you to write down a habit, thought, or belief you want to unlearn and eliminate from your life right now. Ideally, we would like to eliminate every unhealthy habit with a snap of our fingers and live at peace with ourselves. Yet, if we want to experience change, we need to be patient, stay realistic, and be practical. To make things more manageable, let's pick one or two areas you want to work on first. When you improve in these areas, you'll replace it with one or two others, and so on.

As a word of caution, you may experience a few unpleasant emotions while you're working on this exercise, such as frustration, sadness, or anger. Perhaps, your inner critic may emerge and encourage you to stop working on this exercise. It's normal to feel these emotions as you acknowledge the areas you want to unlearn and remove from your life. If these emotions emerge during this exercise, you'll have the opportunity to turn them into healthier, more manageable outcomes. Should you need personal support or a hug, you're welcome to pause and share these feelings with your accountability partner or a loved one.

Keeping in mind your destination, specify how you will commit to unlearn toxic habits and adopt a healthier way of thinking. Go ahead and write down the toxic habits you need to release. Yes, this exercise may be very intense, which is why you have to take the time to do it. Always be honest with yourself. Remember, you can use your journal or the *Diving Deeper* section below.

Once you have listed the areas no longer welcome in your life, you're ready to create a visual picture of what your life will look like once you overcome your struggles and self-induced limitations. To help you get in the zone, I invite you to join me for the following guided visualization exercise. When you're ready, close your eyes and visualize all the benefits no longer having these struggles will bring into your life. How will your life look once you no longer feel limited, fearful, or insecure? Once you unlearn the toxic habit or belief you've adopted, how will you feel? Start writing down what you're seeing as you picture yourself in this ideal situation. Now is a good time to use your sticky notes. Write each benefit on a separate sticky note. Stick them on your wall, desk, studio table, or anywhere you can see them. Surround yourself with goodness and possibilities!

I hope you're feeling excited and hopeful now that you have all those sticky notes everywhere, each listing a benefit of how your state of mind will be or your life will look like once you no longer experience these limitations. Before we keep going, let's take a moment to recap all the work you've been doing so far. By now, you have identified a few unwanted habits and beliefs you are committing to unlearn. You've also visualized a future where your old way of thinking no longer exists and has been replaced with healthier thoughts. How does it make you feel? Write down your feelings and thoughts somewhere around this page or in your wellness journal.

Now, let's turn these struggles into what you truly want to see for yourself. Here is one of the most exciting parts of writing your affirmation. As you write your inner-affirmation, shift your focus from your problems to what you want to see in your life. Use optimistic statements to describe your intentions and a new way of thinking. Express your true emotions and desires and show your passion! Even if you're still experiencing a level of self-doubt, write these statements as if you were feeling 100% confident and trusting yourself fully. Stay hopeful! This way of thinking helps you retrain your mind and convince yourself that, yes, it is possible!

Let me share two examples of areas where people tend to struggle with the most. The first one is mindset blocks. These are self-sabotaging thoughts or limiting beliefs that prevent us from growing personally and professionally. If this is an area you're struggling with at this moment, you can write something like this: *I am no longer listening to* the inner voices that tell me I won't succeed in the art world. I am learning marketing and sales skills that will take my art to the next level.* Perhaps you can choose statements more like this: *I am no longer listening to the inner voices that tell me I cannot be the artist I want to be. I can evolve and become the artist I am meant to be. I'm ready for opportunities!* There you have it! That is how you begin to turn an unhealthy belief into realistic and optimistic thinking.

Another area most people struggle with is fear. If this is the area that needs to be turned around, you can write something like this: *I am no longer letting fear rule my life. I now have the courage I need to overcome the obstacles that may come my way.* When you tell yourself this message day after day, your mind will eventually adopt this way of thinking—even if you don't believe it yet. Consistent repetition can rewire your thinking. As you keep reading these sentences every day, you'll begin to experience positive changes in how you act and think about yourself and others.

Maybe, the first couple of times you read your inner-affirmation, you might think, *This is not how I'm feeling about myself right now.* Perhaps you're not in a good place right now to believe it. It's okay! Feeling that way is quite common, and it doesn't mean there's no hope for you. Whether or not you're feeling it or believing it, my invitation to you is to keep telling yourself these powerful messages every day.

Now is when the magic happens. As you keep bombarding yourself with a healthier way of thinking, you'll end up rewiring your mind and convincing yourself that is your new way of thinking, feeling, and believing. Think about when you wanted to adopt a new positive habit like waking up earlier to work out for an hour. Each time you begin a new routine, you'll probably need some support to make it happen. You'll likely have to set your alarm to wake up earlier. The night before, you might have to set up a reminder on your phone or write a sticky note that reads *workout for an hour tomorrow morning*. You might need reminders every day until getting up to work out becomes second nature to you. Consistent repetition or exposure is the key to adopting a new habit and essential to changing your mental state from self-doubt to self-confidence and from feeling unmotivated to ignited.

It takes time to adopt this new way of thinking. Please, be patient and give yourself some grace. Say you're struggling with insecurity, yet you want to approach a local gallery that represents artists whose art is similar to yours. The voices in your head keep telling you that your art is not good enough for the gallery. As you repeat to yourself that you no longer let insecurities rule your life, guess what will happen to you? You will eventually convince yourself insecurities have no place in your life. You're going to experience a mindset shift as you turn your insecurities into action steps. You'll become courageous and purposeful. Will you experience rejections? Possibly, however, rejections do not define who you are. They're a roadblock along your journey but not who you are. Keep in mind that along a roadblock, there's always a detour. That is why personal affirmations are so helpful for self-motivation and growth. They help you unlearn toxic thinking and replace it with possibilities.

It's time to write down the inner-affirmation paragraph. You're welcome to use the *Diving Deeper* section below or your wellness journal. Remember, the purpose of this paragraph is to help you create visual imagery of how your life will look once you overcome your struggles or self-induced limitations. You will begin to unlearn negative beliefs and replace them with positive thoughts while creating a picture of your ideal self.

An example of how the inner-affirmation paragraph may look like is this:

I am no longer letting fear and insecurities rule my life. I have the courage and grit I need to overcome the obstacles that may come my way. I choose to focus on what truly matters and eliminate unnecessary distractions. I am facing each day with gratitude and an open mind. I will find success and happiness.

Now that you've finished step three, it's time to work on step four, your commitment affirmation. In this section, you will describe your future self. That is, you're describing and manifesting your future. Name what you want to see happening in your life, creative career, or art business. Keep in mind that your purpose doesn't have to be only one thing or remain the same for the rest of your life.

If you're feeling a little bit overwhelmed, I have good news for you! If you've been following the exercises I've been sharing with you in this book, you've started working on this step already! At this point, you have already chosen a goal or destination for yourself. You have also committed to staying focused and working very hard to achieve it. Today, you have a completely different view of yourself as supposed to where you were a few months ago or even before you started reading this book. Where you are today is a step closer to the place you want to be tomorrow.

When it comes to defining our life purpose, sometimes we have in mind one specific idea. What I've learned is we all define purpose differently. Some of us have discovered we have few goals for our lives. Others have identified one sole purpose they want to fulfill. There's nothing wrong with naming one, two, or many purposes. What is important is you have a clear sense of what you are about and the direction you're heading. Circumstances and situations change or evolve as you go through the journey we call life. Therefore, your purpose, commitment, or destination may change or need adjustment based on the season in your life you're currently experiencing. My question to you is, what is your purpose (or purposes) right now? Be mindful that it may change or evolve and be different six months from now, next year, or a few years from now. Be okay with this possibility.

If you have a clear purpose or mission in life, you're good for now. If you're still figuring it out, however, my advice is you take the time to work on this. Don't be too rigid about the purpose or vision of your life and business. As you think about your purpose or mission in life, don't feel stressed out if you cannot come up with it right away. Put this task aside, sit on it for a couple of days, and come back to it as soon as you're able.

I'm not suggesting you procrastinate in this area. I'm inviting you to be flexible, instead, and to give yourself some space to think about this, and practice self-compassion. When you're ready to continue with this exercise, write down on sticky notes or in your journal your expectations and what you're willing to commit to doing to live a happier and more fulfilling life.

A commitment affirmation paragraph may look like this:

Today is full of possibilities. I live expecting to continue growing as a person and evolving in my art career. My purpose at this moment is to influence others in a positive way through the art I make. I commit to begin each day with gratitude and great expectations as I embark on my artistic journey toward healing, happiness, success, and greater creativity. It is possible! As you can see, I wrote "at this moment" because our purpose changes as we change.

Finally, the last step to writing your personal affirmation is to combine the self, inner, and commitment paragraphs into one document. Make sure each section is nicely written and truly reflects your new way of thinking. When you combine the self, inner, and commitment paragraphs you've written, you will have your personal affirmation.

Begin your day by reading your personal affirmation. When you do, you're reminding yourself of your purpose, igniting your motivation, and awakening your passions. It will keep you focused and grounded when things don't go as planned. It will motivate you to rise when you're amid frustration and disappointment. Post this affirmation anywhere you can see it daily. Post it on your refrigerator, or make it a screen saver on your desktop or your phone's wallpaper. It's important you remind yourself why you're doing this, especially during the not so great days. Your life, goals, and accomplishments are important and truly matter.

> **Your life, goals, and accomplishments are important and truly matter.**

Keep repeating to yourself these powerful statements every day until you end up owning and believing them. You'll go from feeling insecure to achieving your goals. You'll arrive at your destination feeling successful and accomplished. I can't stress enough how powerful your personal affirmation can be.

Rather than starting my day with distractions like watching the news, reading emails, or browsing social media, I choose to start my day right by reminding myself of the possibilities available to me. I invite you to do the same! Read your affirmation after you wake up, during breakfast, or while you're practicing meditation. Ask God for help and guidance to make this affirmation your new way of thinking in your prayers. Set yourself up for success by starting your day the right way.

In Sergio's Take, he shares how personal affirmations help him maintain motivation, perspective, and focus during stormy days.

Sergio's Take

Words are powerful. That is something I learned many years ago as I started my art career. I began to write about my thoughts and creative ideas when I was in my second year in college. I was not exactly journaling every day. Rather, I was jotting down thoughts and messages I wanted to remember as an aspiring artist. Sometimes these writings were long and others were single words written on my notepad. I noticed how my words influenced my art-making. I would sit in the studio and read some of these notes. They would come to mind as I was making my art. Then, the artwork began to influence my words while creating an exciting cycle of ideas between words and images. Around that time, I started writing on my art. A lot of paintings began as written verses on the surface of the canvas that I would cover up with paint. Nobody knew there was a whole layer of text and ideas behind the painting. Sometimes, I would let some of the words reveal themselves. At some point, words became so important to me I started writing on top of the art itself. I had found the power of words.

That was in the early '90s before we had cell phones attached to our hands. The internet was not easily accessible by the masses. You may remember the stacks of *Art News* or *Art in America* magazines in most college and university art departments. Professors would bring them so we could read them. That was our internet back then, words written down on sheets of paper. In those days, media was not disruptive as it is today. You had to pick up a magazine, browse it, and decide what you wanted to read. Similarly, you had to turn on the TV and select a channel to watch. You consumed the information you wanted when you wanted.

What a difference from today's world! We are constantly disrupted from our work and creative flow with electronic notifications, texts, messages, or alarms. Algorithms decide what we see. If you think you choose, think again. The software looks at who you are and your browsing patterns. Based on thousands of data points, it predicts what you would like to see and presents it to keep you glued to the screen. That is how the world works today.

What does this technology rant have to do with words or writing? A lot. We write less and read less while we access massive amounts of enticing information in a short period. It is not that words have lost their power. We are simply too distracted to pay attention to them with so many funny cat videos scrolling in our feed. This storm of information makes us feel we can never catch up.

As artists, one day, we are supposed to be posting more on Instagram, and the next, we have to make more videos, jump to TikTok, or start whatever is the newest trend. Before you know it, we have become so distracted simply trying to catch up. I've found this to be true for me in the last few years. Technology is unavoidable if we want to succeed in the world. Not everything is bad. There is also a lot of good. Thanks to our technology and social media platforms, we can connect and grow a community around our art. Somewhere in between this constant disruption, we want to thrive, stay focused, and stay motivated as artists. We want to feel good and live fully.

A few years ago, I heard about the concept of self-affirmations. I remembered the practice I had lost of jotting down my creative thoughts in notebooks. I remembered the power of words and how much they had influenced me in my formation as an artist. At that time, Dr. Yanina was also working on writing her words of affirmation. We both shared ideas and began to exercise this practice of using words to keep us focused, connected to our why, and motivated. Starting this practice was a game-changer for me. There was something special and practical about reading these words every morning before I plugged myself back into the world of technology. The words I selected for myself back then helped me stay focused and gain confidence and strength, particularly when I felt tired or frustrated. They helped me stay focused and grounded in what matters to me.

After adopting this practice, we decided to include it in the Goal Setting System form. I also started to fill up notebooks with notes, ideas, and things I wanted to improve in and out of the studio. After I filled up a notebook, I started a new one. I called my notebooks personal upgrades. Why do I call them personal upgrades? When new software or an app is developed, it is considered version 1.0. Then, as small improvements are ready, you get versions 1.1, 1.2, and so on. Once a major update is ready, then it becomes version 2.0. Software companies make a big deal of it. They begin to announce their major release upgrade before it is even available. We also see this concept with cell phones and many other devices. We all want the newest version because it is better than the last. We all think we have the best one until a new one comes out. It never ends.

I like using this analogy as a self-motivation strategy. Once one of the notebooks is filled up, I release Sergio Gomez 2.0 or whatever number comes next. Each time, I tell my kids, "Hey guys, Sergio's 4.0 is coming out. Get ready! A new me is arriving soon!"

They look at me strangely and say, "You look the same as the previous one."

We laugh about it every time. To this day, I still make a big deal out of it even though my kids are older. Yes, they still have the same reaction. Regardless of their response, I know I am a better and improved version of myself. I feel more equipped and more excited about my new upgrade than the old me. Why? Because that notebook includes my lessons learned, thoughts, ideas, and inspiration that got me to that point in time. Someone once said, it is the greatest failure to be successful and not know how you got there.

You may think this is a silly idea, but it works magic for me. I know I've come a long way when I get to write on the cover with a marker Sergio Gomez version 9.0 (which is the version at the time of this book). Each book gives me a chance to start with a clean slate, reset, and revise my daily affirmations. Are they still true? Do they still hold to this new version of me? Do I need to adjust them? Have I grown tired or numb to these words of affirmation? How can I make my personal affirmation more powerful and meaningful?

That is why I believe this chapter is more than a simple exercise in positive thinking. This chapter is a superpower boost. It can shift your artistic career from boring to exciting once again. It can open your eyes to new dreams. It can start changing the narrative you have believed of yourself and turn it into a beautiful story regardless of your past. Go ahead! Take the time to do the necessary work. Write your affirmations and read them each day. Do not worry how crazy, silly, or whatever they may be. You will share this on social media or make them into a video. The words you write are for your eyes only. Do whatever works for you to trigger your brain to a new you. If you like my little mind game, copy it. If not, come up with something of your own. You do you. Do not worry about what others might think. Your future deserves a new you today.

Diving Deeper

1. Writing your Personal Affirmation.

    You've learned one way to stay motivated is by reminding yourself every day that you matter and your goals and achievements are important. Personal affirmations are an effective strategy to accomplish this. Let's go over the five steps to writing your personal affirmation, mantra, or declaration.

Step 1. Self-Reflection

Before you begin, take time to reflect on what you truly want for yourself and your creative business. It will help to review the prep tips I shared at the beginning of this chapter. Identify who you are and which direction you're heading as a person and creative. Always write your statement in the present tense. Focus on the now.

Remember, when you write your sentences in the present tense, you invite your unconsciousness to work on them immediately. Focus your statements on what you want to see happening for you, not what you are trying to eliminate from your life.

Step 2. Begin your statement by writing the Self-Affirmation section.

Describe who you are, what you have inside you, and your passions. Include your source of life and light. Affirm your current successes, what is going well, positive attributes, and values.

- What fires you up, excites you, and helps you stay focused?

  _____

  _____

- What is your source of life, or what pours out light in your soul?

  _____

  _____

- What are your current successes or wins (small or large)?

  _____

  _____

- What are your positive attributes?

  _____

  _____

- What do you value the most?

  _____

  _____

- What keeps you going during difficult times?

  _____

  _____

Examples:

I am a talented creative person, full of energy, love, and compassion for others.

I have an ability I consider a blessing to myself and those around me.

I love sharing my passion for art-making with others so I can make a difference in my life and those of my loved ones.

I live for (or to) _____.

My source of life and energy comes from _____.

SELF-AFFIRMATION:

_____

_____

_____

Step 3. Write your Inner-Affirmation section.

In this area, we're focusing on your inner struggles. These are mindset blocks, toxic habits, or beliefs that slow you down or discourage you from doing what needs to be done.

- Which habits, thoughts, or beliefs do you want to unlearn and eliminate from your life?
  _____
  _____

- Which emotions are holding you back?
  _____
  _____

- What will you commit to doing to unlearn toxic habits and adopt a healthier way of thinking?
  _____
  _____

Let's change the way you think about these negative areas.

Describe the benefits you will get from no longer having those struggles in your life.

- How will your life look once your self-induced limitations no longer exist?
  _____
  _____

- How will you feel once you unlearn the toxic habit or belief you've adopted?
  _____
  _____

As you write your inner-affirmation, shift the focus from your problems to what you want to see happening in your life. Describe your intentions using positive and real statements. Express your true emotions and desires and show your passion!

Examples:

Struggle: Mindset Blocks

- I am no longer listening to the inner voices that tell me I won't succeed in the art world. I am instead learning marketing and sales skills that will take my art to the next level.

Struggle: Fear

- I am no longer letting fear rule my life. I have the courage and grit to overcome the obstacles that may come my way.

INNER-AFFIRMATION:

_____
_____
_____

Step 4. Write your Commitment Affirmation section.

Identify your purpose (s) in life as of today. Keep in mind it doesn't have to be one purpose. It will likely evolve based on the season you experience.

- What expectations do you have for yourself?
  _____
  _____

- What are you willing to commit to doing to make your expectations a reality?
  _____
  _____

- What can you do right now to live a fulfilling life?
  _____
  _____

Examples:

- I promise to face each day with gratitude and an open mind.
- I live expecting to continue growing as a person and evolving as an artist.
- I commit to focus on my growth and reject distractions that may come my way.
- My purpose is to influence others in a positive way through the art I make.

COMMITMENT AFFIRMATION:
_____
_____
_____

Step 5. Put Together Your Personal Affirmation

Finally, let's put the *Self*, *Inner*, and *Commitment* affirmations together to create your Personal Affirmation. Enjoy every moment as you write your affirmation.

_____'s (insert your name)
PERSONAL AFFIRMATION

_____

_____

_____

_____

Wrapping It Up

Congratulations for taking the time to create this affirmation that reflects your unique needs, desires, hopes, expectations, and purpose! You've taken a significant step toward your healing. Print and post it where you can see it every day. You can also make it available on your phone. Start your day by reading it and reminding yourself that your life, goals, and accomplishments are meaningful and truly matter. I hope your personal affirmation will help you stay motivated and focused as you work toward arriving at your next destination in life.

Now might be a good time to schedule a time to meet with your accountability partner and share your reaction to this chapter. When you're ready, let's move on to the last chapter of this book. In Chapter Eight, you'll learn ways to adopt healthy patterns that lead to living life to its fullest.

CHAPTER EIGHT
DETOXIFYING AND LIVING MY LIFE TO THE FULLEST

An artist friend whom we haven't seen for a few years attended one of Sergio's solo exhibitions. She was telling me about the events she's involved with and all the committees on which she volunteers. She also mentioned that her art career has become a side gig because she doesn't have time to build her business. As a result, she had to get a part-time job while she gets her art business organized.

With sadness in her eyes, she said, "I want to dedicate more time to my art career, but it's complicated! Between keeping up with the needs and wants of those around me, trying to figure out how to run my art career, make art, and my part-time job, I don't have enough hours in a day to grow my art business. I can't seem to find a balance between my personal life, art career, and enjoying life. I'm always running around."

Does this sound familiar? Often, we fall for the busyness trap without realizing it. We live in a culture that glorifies busyness. Everyone seems to be very busy these days. Somehow, busyness has become a trophy or a gold medal people wear proudly. The line between busyness and productiveness seems blurry. I've lost track of the number of times people tell me how busy they are running around nonstop doing "things." Busyness doesn't necessarily translate into productivity. If we aren't careful, we may end up polluting our lives or simply going with the flow and living without purpose or intention.

Probably, the only positive outcome from the Covid-19 pandemic is that it forced us to stop. We were forced to stay put to lower the spread of the virus. There were lockdowns and restrictions everywhere-no running around, traveling, appointments, distractions, volunteering, or going places. To some, this was a shocking reality. To others, being still was needed and welcomed. I was one of those who appreciated being still. It helped me put my life in perspective, reassess my goals, reinvent myself, focus on what truly matters in my life and reevaluate my relationships. During that time, I was able to clarify the purpose of this book, its topics, and its impact on creatives like you. Being still also reminded me about the importance of finding a healthy balance that makes sense for me and the value of living my life to the fullest.

When we aren't living our lives to the fullest, we feel overwhelmed, stressed, and tense. We are not ourselves. We are less patient, less tolerant, and more irritable. As a result, we might not be in the right state of mind to make the best decisions for ourselves or our art business. On the other hand, when our state of mind is healthy and we can find harmony among our many responsibilities, we can face challenges more objectively, become productive, choose self-care, make a difference, and live purposefully.

We hear over and over about finding balance in life. After all, we want to be healthy and happy. That sounds great, but what on earth does it mean? Are we talking about splitting ourselves or our time in half or three-quarters? Is it about dedicating 50% of our time to everything related to living our lives and the other 50% to art-making? Is this possible? Perhaps some artists can wing it, but, for most, the 50/50 concept is unreal.

A healthy balance is something only you can define. What looks like a balanced life for me might not even be close to what a healthy balance may look like for you. The key is to take time to reflect on and decide where your time, energy, and effort will be invested based on the season of life you're currently living. To some, a balanced life involves family, art-making, growing their art business, and investing in self-care. To others, caring for an elderly parent or raising children takes most of their time; therefore, building their art business may be a side gig at this moment. Be willing to embrace balance as changeable based on the season you're currently living instead of seeing it as a strict 50/50 concept.

A healthy balance is something only you can define.

Let's start by clarifying what I don't mean when I refer to a healthy balance. It's impossible to divide your life into two equal parts and function properly. A healthy balance does not require you to place your life's circumstances on one side of the scale and your art career on the other, so there's equal weight on both sides. The truth is, both areas intertwine and may co-exist harmoniously even when the demands are different. One area affects and influences the other. It is unrealistic and unfair to you to divide your complex life into two equal parts in hopes of experiencing some sort of balance. If we want to experience a level of balance and harmony in our lives, however, we have to detoxify our lives first. In this chapter, I invite you to explore a more realistic approach to what balance looks like in a healthy lifestyle. Together, we'll figure out what makes sense for you as we go over five practical strategies you can use to detoxify and live your life to the fullest.

The first strategy to detoxify your life and live to the fullest is to define what is important to you. It's not about other people's agendas and what they want to impose on you. It is about taking the time to define and acknowledge what matters to you. Most of us have many responsibilities, and, at times, it feels as if there are not enough hours in a day to accomplish what we need to do.

When you take time to outline what you do each day and how much time you dedicate to each thing you do, you might realize that often, we misuse our time on things that aren't important or aligned to our agenda. Consequently, we may be busy but not necessarily productive. Is it possible you're overcommitting and spreading yourself too thin? Are you volunteering for a committee because they need someone to fill the position, but the commitment is not aligned with your goals? Maybe your children are involved in sports, after-school programs, or extracurricular events, and you're constantly driving them around town. Is it possible friends and family keep asking of you and taking over your time? Could you be spending a significant amount of time browsing social media or binging on movies and television series? Are you finding yourself constantly busy catering to others and being pulled away from what truly matters to you?

My dear reader, I invite you to identify what's important to you right now, in the current season of your life. Maybe bringing food to the table or strengthening your relationship with a significant other is at the top of your priority list. Perhaps you're ready to build a profitable art business and take your art career to the next level, yet the busyness of life is distracting you from moving forward. Take a moment to write down the areas you're identifying as important. You can always use your sticky notes or head to the *Diving Deeper* section to write down your list.

Once you identify what is important to you, you're ready for my second strategy, which is to be selective. Let me start by saying it's okay to say no! If someone told you in the past that saying no is rude, don't believe it! If you're constantly busy, yet you're neglecting yourself and loved ones and not seeing results, something has to change.

Let's acknowledge that balancing your personal life and art career isn't simple or easy. Remember, it's not about a 50/50 split where 50% goes to investing in your life and 50% to accomplishing your professional goals. It's about finding inner peace and satisfaction with how you're handling and investing your time. Each season in life has its temporary priorities. What's imperative today might not be as important a few months from now. If you're not focusing on what is important right now, you'll end up feeling as if you're running on a hamster wheel with no purpose or destination.

In the investment industry, assets have value and future benefits. Without a complex financial lesson, assets are used to produce positive economic value, such as cash flow. You won't throw your assets out the window. You probably manage your assets intelligently to receive greater value in return. I've learned to treat time as one of my most valuable assets. When time is used wisely, it can work wonders for you. Since time can't be regained, you have a choice to make. Are you going to take control of your time or allow others to control it for you?

As you begin to treat time as an asset, you will guard it wisely. Starting today, you will no longer say yes to every invitation others present to you. You're going to be selective and think like a serious investor. Measure the investment and benefits of each invitation. Ask yourself these questions: *Is this invitation or commitment contributing to my personal and professional growth? What are the pros and cons of committing? What impact will this invitation make in my relationship with loved ones if I accept it? Is it worth it?*

Once you become selective about your time and what you're allowing in your schedule, you'll begin to differentiate between what's important and what can wait or be rejected. You'll begin to declutter your schedule and make space to seize opportunities that lead to your development. If you don't make space, success will not find you. Your actions and decisions should focus on nurturing the areas you identified to be important. That means you begin to choose to invest your time, effort, and energy in accomplishing what is important to you, and no longer allow other people's agendas to run your schedule. As you begin to say no to activities, commitments, or events not in alignment with your plans, you'll begin to experience a sense of peace, self-satisfaction, and harmony between your personal life and art career.

> **If you don't make space, success will not find you.**

By no means am I criticizing volunteer work or getting involved in collective efforts. As citizens of this world, it's our responsibility to give back and help others. Sergio and I are involved in organizations and support causes that are important to us. The difference is we do it when we can dedicate time for it, not because we feel guilty or obligated to be involved. There was a time when our schedules were booked with other people's agendas. It wasn't pretty. We learned our lesson and want to pass it on to you. We no longer allow people to impose their agendas on us. We have become very selective about the way we invest our time. Time is priceless, and it can't be regained. Saying no to invitations not aligned with our goals, passions, and values has become easier. Most importantly, we choose not to allow feelings of guilt or obligation to influence our decisions.

Overscheduled lives can potentially lead to psychological, emotional, or physiological breakdowns. The busier we become, the less time we have to invest in self-care. The less we care about ourselves, the easier it is to experience mental and physical challenges. Don't fall into this trap. I invite you to take control of your time and invest it responsibly and in things that truly matter. No longer allow others to impose their agendas on you.

Let's move on to my third strategy: defining healthy balance based on your current life season. As I've mentioned before, there will be seasons when your life rhythm gets out of balance. It happens! Be mindful about this, and know what you are sacrificing in the bargain. Once you achieve your goals, things get done, or the support arrives, make sure to get back into balance as quickly as possible.

A healthy balance is experiencing harmony between life, family, career, and relationships. Different things that require your attention are happening simultaneously, and you are in tune with each of them. Some need more attention than others. This is normal. Again, to enjoy harmony and balance in your life, it's important you choose to invest your time, energy, and effort in what matters to you. Measure the impact this investment is making in your life and those around you and make tough choices so you're able to experience the inner peace that comes with doing what's right. Something that has helped me find harmony is accepting that it's unrealistic to do everything all the time. Each season in life brings its circumstances, and priorities may change temporarily. Struggles, challenges, and hurdles may come your way. It's part of life. As you assess situations before you invest in them, filter them out, and eliminate the habits and relationships that bring you down, you'll soon experience harmony and peace of mind.

As the years pass, we are presented with circumstances that help us grow or slow us down. As much as we are intentional about keeping harmony, there will be times when life will bombard us with lemons. You'll likely experience what I call a temporary imbalance. As frustrating and upsetting as this may be, it's important you see it as a temporary circumstance or season. There are times when temporary imbalances and sacrifices must be made for our growth and the well-being of our loved ones.

There's no need to feel guilty when your time, energy, and effort have to be channeled toward a specific circumstance or an unexpected responsibility during a season. We must work toward not making it a permanent situation. When Sergio and I founded the Art NXT Level Academy, we faced a temporary imbalance. We channeled our time, energy, focus, and effort toward developing and growing the Art NXT Level Academy. We were selective about accepting invitations from others and put on hold indulging things to focus on building a sustainable business that has been making a difference in the lives of thousands of artists from all over the world. We invested our time in our children and the Academy during that season. We were clear that it was a temporary imbalance, and we were intentional about not neglecting our health and the people who matter to us. We kept our eyes on the prize always working toward restoring balance once again.

Maybe you were invited to have a solo exhibition at your local art museum. You excitedly accepted the invitation, which means you're experiencing a priority shift. Your focus now is to prepare for the solo exhibition. You asked yourself the assessment questions I shared in my previous strategy and concluded this commitment would contribute significantly to the growth of your art career. It's a go!

Consequently, your family, relationships, responsibilities, and social life will be affected temporarily. Maybe you'll be getting home late and missing dinner time with the family for a while. Perhaps you'll find yourself passing on social activities because you have to prepare your work and have it ready before the deadline. You'll experience a temporary imbalance, yet it will make a positive impact on your life in the long run. Saying no to others might be upsetting or uncomfortable, but it needs to be done for the sake of your well-being and progress. Once the exhibition is over, you'll be able to have dinner with your family again and resume your social life.

Maybe you're presently caring for an elderly parent, and your studio time has been significantly affected. Between making meals and taking your parent from one medical appointment to another, there's not much time left to spend in your studio. Perhaps you recently became a new parent, and, for obvious reasons, your art practice is slowing down. The list can go on and on. As you adjust to these changes, keep in mind that what requires attention today might require less attention a few months or years from now. Always have a plan to get back on track!

I encourage you to label these unexpected or short-term circumstances as a temporary imbalance. Otherwise, they can potentially become your new normal. Be conscious and proactive about not neglecting the people and things that matter to you. Stay focused. Remind yourself why you're experiencing the temporary imbalance and what needs to happen to end it.

Balance is not about leveling the playing field. Sometimes, decisions that are not equally distributed or ideal have to be made, yet they benefit you and your loved ones. You'll experience balance and harmony when you no longer fight and blame yourself for your current season of life. You choose instead to embrace each season in life. Invest your time, energy, and effort wisely during your current season in life. Evaluate the impact this investment is making on you and those around you, and make necessary changes so you can experience the inner peace that comes with doing what's right.

Good times are always treasured, but rough times will also come. Challenges and changes will happen, and adjustments will have to be made. When life gives you lemons, make art. Avoid falling into a negative thinking trap by remaining optimistic and open-minded. Rather than fighting season changes, learn to dance with them. If your current season demands it, be willing to make temporary adjustments and sacrifices for your growth and the well-being of your family. Whether it is spending less time with your extended family, saying no to friends, cutting down expenses, or stepping down from commitments, don't let guilt distract or blind you.

A temporary imbalance must have an end. Be intentional about not letting imbalance become the norm in your life. Stay focused and remind yourself why you're doing this. As you honor yourself, you'll begin to find inner peace with the new way you're handling and investing in your life.

My fourth strategy to live to the fullest is building and nurturing a strong support system. Research has shown meaningful relationships are essential to be happy, successful, and live a fulfilling life.[2] Authentic relationships make our life's journey more exciting. When we surround ourselves with people who truly have our interests in mind, we feel loved, accepted, and supported.

People are meant to be around other people. Friendships can help us grow, thrive, and survive. We have an innate need to belong and be together with those who matter to us. There's something special about belonging. When you belong, you experience a sense of peace and feel safe, seen, and heard. If you have a strong support system, you know how friendships can enrich our lives. Good friends encourage us to make good decisions, like replacing bad eating habits, starting an exercise routine, or practicing meditation. Healthy relationships can also lift us, push us to be better, and support us along the way. Life is more joyful, and it can feel like anything is possible when we're surrounded by authentic friends.

I am a true believer in intentionally building the right inner circle for ourselves. One way to do this is by investing in relationships that are truthful and align with who we are. I'm not expecting each person in my inner circle to think or be exactly like me. I appreciate having people smarter than me who cut to the chase, challenge me, and tell me the real deal. I also appreciate those who are the voice of reason—even when I may not always like what they have to say—and support me throughout my journey. I don't focus on quantity as much as I do on quality. I'm very intentional about staying away from those constantly in turmoil or who have serious drama in their lives, as they only bring unnecessary chaos. I prefer to invest my time nurturing and strengthening a few supportive, genuine relationships than spreading myself too thin trying to please a wide variety of acquaintances. By no means am I suggesting having many friends is bad. Some people invest in many relationships and prefer to have a larger support system. We all have unique needs.

There was a time when our inner circle was toxic. Sergio and I allowed a few people with toxic hidden agendas to sneak into it. We soon learned the value of becoming very selective about who belongs in our inner circle. Maybe you realize your inner circle is not in good standing. The good news is you can do something about it. It is never too late to detoxify your inner circle and build a healthy support system for yourself. When you invest in the right people, blessings will come upon you. It's a ripple effect!

Let me share a few tips to help you cleanse your inner circle. Intentionally, surround yourself with genuine, optimistic people who will be there for you during your triumphs and also the not-so-great days. You don't have to share the same perspectives or opinions. Different perspectives help you challenge yourself and think about other possibilities or alternatives. Authentic friendships are there for you, push you to meet your goals, and help you become the best version of yourself. It is not a one-way approach. You have to make yourself available, show up, and support others as well. As you adopt a giving mindset, where you give as much or more as you receive, your relationships will grow stronger. The best friendships are two-way relationships where both parties nurture, encourage, and support one another based on their unique attributes and gifts.

The truth is many of us are dealing with unhealthy relationships. Maybe there's someone in your life who drains you, drags you down, or is poisoning your soul. If you aren't mindful, you may find yourself letting their harmful comments poison your mind. When we are surrounded by toxic relationships consuming our time and energy, we stop trying. We begin to believe these hurtful words are true. We assume we are not good enough, our art is not good enough, or we're not young enough to keep up with the changes in technology.

I call this type of people relational vampires. They suck up your time, energy, and resources without mercy. They always have an agenda in mind that only benefits them. They invite you for coffee or lunch to pick your brains. We have declined so many of these invitations. They take as much as they can from you and spread negative energy everywhere they go. Often, these are one-way relationships that only lead to disappointment, frustration, and headaches. Relational vampires constantly complain, criticize your choices, and expect you to meet their needs. Unfortunately, stakes, crosses, sunlight, or stuffing their mouth with garlic won't keep them away. If a few names are popping in your head as you're reading this chapter, they're likely the relational vampires roaming in your personal space.

There's a difference between acquaintances and friendships, especially when referring to our support system. The word friend has been distorted by social media platforms where we can claim to have hundreds of friends even when we have never met most of them in person. Authentic friendships are more profound and intimate than acquaintances or social media friends. I invite you to assess your inner circle. Is it based on genuineness or superficial relationships?

Today is detox day one if you have relational vampires in your inner circle. As long as these individuals stick around, their negative energy will bring unnecessary stress into your life. You don't need this burden in your life right now. You've learned your time is a valuable asset that cannot be wasted. Don't allow your relational vampires to steal your time and pull you into their agendas. Today is the day you begin to let go of relationships that are putting you down, clouding your purpose, and wasting your time.

Let's get real. I know this may be easier said than done. I've been there. It is difficult, but it is possible. There are toxic relationships that can be dissolved immediately, whereas others need some transition time. There are also circumstances when a relationship can't be fully dissolved. I get it! They can be downgraded by pursuing it less and limiting sharing of personal information. You can choose how much time you're willing to invest in this relationship and at what level you will be influenced by it. If the other person is willing to hear you out, share with them the reasons why you believe the relationship is changing.

You can start the conversation by saying, "I appreciate your friendship, but I feel like I need to focus on the plans I've set for myself this year."

Perhaps you could say, "I also feel like our lives are following different paths." Focus the conversation on how you feel, not what the other person has done wrong. If the person is likely not to listen or accept what you are saying, gradually reduce social interaction with them until the relationship fades away. Set clear boundaries. You don't have to answer every text or phone call from this person. You don't need to accept each invitation from this person either.

Let's take a moment to assess your inner circle. How do you describe your inner circle? Can you say each person is supportive? Are you surrounded by genuine people who bring out the best in you or relational vampires who suck up every drop of energy from your life? Use your sticky notes or journal to write down your notes. We'll take some time to reflect on these questions in the *Diving Deeper* section below. Always be selective about whom you welcome in your inner circle.

The fifth and last strategy is to invest in self-care; this is one of my favorites to teach. I strongly believe that to optimize our potential and become the best version of ourselves, we must invest in self-care. Each time I travel in an airplane, the flight attendant goes over a safety demonstration before takeoff. They cover the items listed on the safety card, share a few in-flight announcements, and provide demonstrations so we can be somewhat prepared in case of an emergency landing. What do they usually tell you to do when it comes to the air mask?

If you're traveling with a child or someone who requires assistance, secure your mask on first, and then assist the other person.

There's a reason why you have to put on your mask first before you help others. Supposed you experience a serious disturbance at a high altitude and fail to put on your mask first. In that case, you risk quickly becoming unconscious from lack of oxygen, hence unable to assist others. This example illustrates the importance of taking care of ourselves so we are better able to optimize our creativity, fulfill our purpose(s), and make a difference in the life of others.

You and I are very complex individuals with a mind, body, and soul. Each of these three areas is interconnected, and one influences the others. When your body hurts, your mind and soul are affected. When your mind or soul hurts, your body reacts to this disruption. Therefore, to experience balance or harmony in your life, you must see yourself as an individual whose parts or areas intertwine to make you whole. As you begin to see your mind, body, and soul as one, you understand the value of prioritizing all of them.

We constantly make decisions—about personal matters, our loved ones, our art business, financial issues, etc. you name it. One of the best decisions I've ever made is to invest in self-care so I can better face hurdles and challenges that may come my way while maintaining a level of self-control. I can't stress this enough. When we aren't healthy, we lose our patience, get irritated quickly, and become intolerable. We don't give ourselves space to reflect on the situation and make poor decisions. Often, our loved ones end up paying for it. Don't let life get in your way to recharge yourself. At the end of the day, what good will it do to have an exhausted, sick, and miserable you around? Not much! We need you to have the focus, energy, and inspiration to continue creating amazing art.

To avoid reaching the miserable level, consider my three wellness tweaks that can dramatically improve the quality of your life. They target your mind, body, and soul. My first tweak is to take care of your body. You only have one body until the end of your journey. Take good care of it. It's no secret that when we neglect our physical health, we're sabotaging our quality of life and our mental health. If this is an area where you are ahead of the game, congratulations. Keep it up. If you're telling yourself, *Yikes,*

I've been neglecting my physical health lately, today is the day you choose to prioritize it. Schedule your annual wellness checkups. Take an honest look at your eating habits. If you are consuming unhealthy foods like processed meats, sugary drinks, junk food, snacks high in salt and sugar, saturated fats, or excessive alcohol often, it's time to slow down and replace them with healthier choices. It's never too late to rewire your brain, unlearn unhealthy habits, and replace them with better ones. Commit to making healthy physical and dietary choices.

Good sleep habits are also essential in a healthy lifestyle. There are so many benefits to consistent sleep. It helps your body heal and repair. It also recharges your body, leaving you refreshed and alert when you wake up. Sleep is also essential in brain function. As your body is resting, it's boosting your concentration, problem-solving, and productivity. One of my secrets to improving cognitive functioning, staying alert, and being in a better mood during the day is taking power naps. I take a power nap when my body asks for it without feeling guilty about it. These are short naps taken during the day. They usually last about 15-30 minutes. If you're a parent of little ones or teenagers, you know how much they love and need naps to help them recharge and function. Adults also need naps. Sergio and I can attest to this truth. The lesson here is, get enough sleep!

Indeed, I must address daily physical activity. We are not skipping this one. On a serious note, we are responsible for taking good care of our bodies, and daily physical activity is a must. I'm not asking you to train for a marathon. I'm asking you to add moderate physical activity to your daily routine. Whether you follow the ultimate workout routine, walk thirty minutes a day, or practice yoga, regular exercising has unlimited benefits. It lowers your risk of developing some diseases, improves your muscle strength, boosts your endurance, eases tension, and improves sleep, among many other benefits. Create a physical activity routine that works for you. Try your best to stay consistent. Avoid staying seated in your studio chair for long consecutive hours. Set up a reminder a few times a day to get up and walk around. Do a few stretching exercises while you are in your studio or office. There are many health apps you can use to help you keep track of your physical activity (or lack thereof). Use them! If physical health is an area that needs attention in your life, start your journey by speaking with your medical doctor or nurse practitioner. Move your body and stay active throughout the day. You won't regret this decision.

Mental and physical health are equally important to enjoy a healthier lifestyle, leading me to my second wellness tweak, which is to focus on your mental health. When you invest in your emotional and psychological well-being, you're better able to handle stress, focus, be productive, relate to others, and make healthier choices. I'll be the first to congratulate you for already tweaking this area in your life. You've been scheduling time to read this book. You've also been working diligently on the inner-reflection exercises in the *Diving Deeper* section of each chapter. You're actively investing in your mental health.

It's no secret mental health affects how we feel, think, and act. When unresolved issues and unpleasant emotions linger in our psyche, our psychological well-being, creativity, and overall state of mind suffer. Emotions are essential in our daily living. The way you react, take action, and face obstacles is often influenced by your emotional state. If you're feeling optimistic and confident, you'll likely make better decisions or react more proactively to an unexpected situation than if you're feeling stressed, sad, or confused. Even in situations where you believe your decisions are guided by pure logic, emotions are present. They influence our decisions and how we interpret words from others, experiences, and circumstances.

The benefits of taking care of our mental health are endless. When you do, you feel alive and excited. You're able to manage stress and remain focused on what matters to you the most. You're more in tune with your loved ones, art, creativity, and purpose. When you feel good, confident, and optimistic, you can handle the ups and downs of life in a better way. The more connected you are with your emotional well-being, the more you're able to cope with adversity and adapt to changes in your life.

When the going gets tough, don't keep it to yourself, hoping the difficulty will magically disappear. Share your troubles with trusted people in your life such as your accountability partner and your inner circle. Talking about it may help you put things in perspective and feel you're not alone. We all need an emotional support system in our lives. Life is fuller when you share it with others. At the same time, as much as we love the support of others, we can't rely only on them for motivation. You've been learning self-motivation strategies in this book. Keep them handy. It's our responsibility to make the necessary changes to improve the quality of our life.

Maybe you're facing a situation that requires making a life-changing decision. Perhaps you need to find a new studio because it is causing distress, or you're considering moving to another town, state, or country in your search for a better quality of life. There are times when big decisions must be made for the sake of our physical and mental well-being. We aren't meant nor equipped to live in distress, misery, and chaos our entire lives. It's okay to sacrifice some things for the sake of a greater quality of life and healthier long-term benefits. Don't let the what-ifs and feelings of guilt cloud your mind. It's about weighing the pros and cons of each choice and deciding which ones will improve the quality of your life. If you're facing a life-changing decision, you'll find exercises in the *Diving Deeper* area to help you make a sound decision.

You deserve to live a healthier, happier, and more meaningful life. You have desires and dreams you want to see come true. You want to experience peace of mind and harmony in your life. You can have all this! It is possible. Invest in your emotional wellness, and address the triggers and wounds you've been carrying for so long.

> **You deserve to live a healthier, happier, and more meaningful life.**

Keep in mind that mental health can change over time when the demands placed on us exceed our coping abilities and resources. For this reason, it's important it becomes a priority, and you are intentional about caring for your mental health. If this is an area that needs professional support in your life, start your journey by speaking with a mental health professional. Together you'll decide the most appropriate treatment plan based on your needs and circumstances, including any biological factors or chemical imbalances in the brain.

My last wellness tweak to improve the quality of your life is to dedicate time to nurture your soul. Have you ever felt disconnected or an emptiness inside you can't quite pinpoint? Maybe this is a sign your soul needs attention. We add to our schedules important events we don't want to miss. If you have an art opening or artist talk, you surely add it to your schedule. If you're like me, you'll also set a reminder because you don't want to miss it. I encourage you to do the same with your soul. Add soul-time to your calendar and set a reminder until it becomes your daily routine.

Soul-time is simply a moment in the day where you focus on nurturing your soul. We are spiritual beings. Deep inside, we know there's something greater than us. Our souls long to connect with our Creator or tune in to our sense of spirit. By no means am I trying to convince you to find religion. It is not about that. I'm inviting you to stay connected with your source of life and light. Soul-time allows you to nurture your soul while also attending to your mind and body. It doesn't have to be complicated. Simplicity goes a long way! The more complicated you make it, the greater the likelihood you'll find an excuse to skip it.

In my case, I'm intentional about starting my day by nurturing my soul. I don't start my day by connecting to the outside world, checking my emails, or social media accounts. I begin instead by making myself a hot double-espresso latte that I enjoy while I'm doing my devotions. As someone who follows Christ's teachings, I believe God is my Creator. As a spiritual practice, I take time in the morning to connect with God. I nurture this spiritual connection through reading the Bible, prayer, and meditation. There's a sense of peace that fills my soul and sets the right tone to begin the day.

There are many ways to nurture your soul. Perhaps you will do something similar or completely different. You may find a spiritual connection to nature or have spiritual beliefs different from mine. Maybe your soul longs for authentic human connections. What matters is you take the time to nurture your soul as much as you nurture your body and mind.

Another simple way to lift your soul is by adding joyful moments to your day that keep in tune with your soul and well-being. Joyful moments are simple things you can do daily to keep you feeling grateful for your life, what you have, who you are, and your loved ones. During the day, I do my best to add a few more joyful moments to my day, like enjoying a glass of wine while watching the sunset or working on my mazes book to exercise my brain. I love watching the moon at night. I tend to peek out to have a glimpse of it every night. It reminds me of the greatness of creation and how there's so much more than meets the eye. I end my day with prayer and a guided relaxation meditation or breathing exercise to prime my mind, body, and soul to rest. There are days when things get crazy, and I can only experience a joyful moment or two. It's fine. What is important here is to prioritize and do your best to have a daily joyous moment that reminds you you're alive and helps you stay connected with your soul.

My dear reader, what are you doing to nurture your soul? Maybe it is through prayer, meditation, going for a walk to enjoy nature, hiking, or reading a book. Let me share with you a few ideas to add to your repertoire.

- Take time to engage in your spiritual practice, whether through prayer, devotions, attending a place of worship, connecting with nature, or any way you choose to practice.
- Wake up early to watch the sunrise or enjoy the night sky while having a glass of full-bodied wine.
- Keep a gratitude journal. Every day write down one thing you're grateful for.
- Jot down your thoughts in the morning or before going to bed, even if you have to write, *I have nothing to say*.
- Visit local beaches, rivers, lakes, mountain trails, nature parks, or gardens.
- Practice relaxation techniques like stretching and breathing exercises to nurture your inner-self during the day.
- Send random inspiring text messages to loved ones and friends. Their reactions will fill your heart with joy!

- Bake or cook something special for yourself or someone. Each time you do something for someone else, your soul gets an instant boost.
- Call a friend you haven't talked to in a while.
- Use a foot massage roller, handheld massager, back and neck massager, scalp massagers, or other self-therapeutic tools to release your body's tension and help you relax.

You get the point. I want to invite you to be intentional about adding soul-time to your day through spiritual practices and joyful moments. I function well with structure and routines. Maybe too much structure is not your thing. Maybe, you're more a spur-of-the-moment type of person. You don't need to be highly structured to nourish your soul. If the schedule idea is too overwhelming, set up a reminder. Above all, be intentional about making it happen. Otherwise, you'll get distracted, and the day will end without having your soul-time.

When you're intentional about refueling your mind, body, and soul, you'll enjoy the benefits of healthy living. You will make better decisions for yourself and your art career. You'll be more optimistic, alert, and patient. You'll optimize your creativity while avoiding feeling burned out. We need a healthy and dependable you. Prioritizing your well-being is the best investment you can make for yourself and your loved ones!

It's time to move on to Sergio's Take. Check out what he has to say about how detoxifying and living your life to the fullest can impact your creativity and art business. Next, take some time to work on the reflective exercises I prepared for you in the *Diving Deeper* section. You're almost done with this journey. Let's finish strong!

Sergio's Take

It was a cold winter morning. As I was on my way to teach a full day of classes at the college where I worked, I began to feel a little strange. I thought it was the cold weather. Winter is not my favorite season. I hate cold temperatures, particularly January and February, because they're the coldest months in Chicago. As I drove into the parking lot on the main campus, I began to feel lightheaded all of a sudden. In a matter of seconds, everything started to spin around me. It was as if I was in the center, and the world was spinning around me extremely rapidly—so fast that I lost control of my sense of space. I could not tell left from right, up from down. I was in the middle of a severe vertigo attack. I had never experienced something like this before.

I thought I was having a heart attack or a seizure episode. I stopped the car by the campus entrance. Fortunately, the campus police saw me and came to see what was happening. They immediately called an ambulance. All I remember is waking up in a hospital bed a couple of hours later with Dr. Yanina by my side. It was a hell of an experience. My first reaction was to thank God it did not happen while I was driving on the expressway. I could have hurt myself badly and probably others. It all happened so quickly.

I was released after spending a few hours in the Emergency Room. They recommended following up with my primary care physician for further evaluation. I was still disoriented and not exactly in good balance. These vertigo episodes started to reappear approximately every week or so for the span of a few months. Each time I had an episode, I was down for about 24 to 48 hours before I could regain my balance to stand up by myself or walk. For a while, I was not able to drive a car. I also experienced difficulty focusing my eyes on things. I'm not talking about a minor inconvenience but a debilitating condition. I was afraid and confused, trying to stay afloat and not lose my new teaching job.

After many specialists, treatments, and expensive brain and inner ear studies, the doctors believed it was a viral infection that found its way through my weak immune system, causing permanent damage to my inner ear. Consequently, I developed an ongoing condition I have to this day. I have lost some hearing and suffer from tinnitus. During this difficult time, a friend told me about acupuncture. I was at a point I would do anything to find relief. To my surprise, acupuncture was the only treatment that has kept the vertigo episodes far and apart. It is now a year or two in-between an episode occurrence. That is a huge improvement! I can say I have pulled my life back together thanks to God, the treatments, and the support of my family, but it has not been easy. I still suffer the consequences of this condition.

Why do I bring this sad story to my last contribution to this book? Looking back, it was stress that weakened my immune system. I was caught in a bad place. You see, six months before this happened, I had recently landed a tenure-track teaching position at a local college, which is something that, as you may know, is hard to find. Tenured positions are the best opportunity in higher education. Once you get tenured, you can stay there until you retire. It means job security. As you can imagine, I was very excited. Yet, it was the first time I taught each of the courses assigned to my teaching schedule. I had spent the last five years working in a fast-paced design and marketing agency and occasionally teaching an evening class to gain experience. I went into teaching without lesson plans. Each night, I had to create the lesson for the classes I was going to teach the next day. I was sleeping very little during the whole first year of teaching. It was rough.

On top of that, we had a one-year-old baby. My wife was also working full-time as a psychologist, and we had only recently moved to a bigger house. A lot was going on in my life. I was trying to unpack, teach, and manage family life. Outside of that, in my artist's life, I was running and managing our new gallery, organizing shows, and preparing for my exhibitions. Everything was piling on me to the point of exhaustion. I was not taking good care of myself. My immune system was compromised. When this happened, everything came to a standstill for me. Today, I am still dealing with the consequences of neglecting my health during that temporary imbalance in my life.

Like Dr. Yanina said, when life gives you lemons, make art. After six months of not touching a brush, I began to make art again. My priority was to recover and function back in the world. Over the years, there have been ups and downs with my vertigo condition. I've noticed how much stress influences my state of health. When I am getting overwhelmed and stressed out, I feel it in my ears and my balance. These feelings remind me to slow down and take care of myself—to relax, take time to breathe, and do "me time" to regain balance.

You may wonder why in the world do I keep doing so many things? After almost twenty years of living with this condition, I have come to understand my limits. I know what I can handle and what I can't. I have learned to say no and be okay with it. By default, I am a yes type of guy. I used to say yes to everything. Not anymore. My yeses are far in-between. People come to me with ideas, projects, and things they would like me to be part of. I'm no longer afraid to say no. I'm no longer afraid of missing out. We have to permit ourselves to say no, to disappoint others, and leave opportunities on the table to live a healthier and more fulfilled life.

The journey back to a healthier me has also taught me about cleaning up my inner circle and staying away from relational vampires, as Dr. Yanina puts it. They no longer have space in my life. It does not mean I don't care about other people. I love building community and bringing people together. It is one of my passions and strengths. It is also why I have built a beautiful community inside the Art NXT Level Academy with artists from around the world. I have become cautious and selective about who belongs in my inner circle and who has influence over my life.

Back to my story. After ten years, I said goodbye to my tenured teaching position. As much as I enjoyed working with students, I had to let go of the security of a job in exchange for building my art business. I resigned and have never looked back. I now enjoy working on my art career, running the gallery, curating, and coaching. Each day has a little bit of all these areas. Some days one needs more attention than the others, but I enjoy all aspects of my business. There have been many challenges along the way to this point. I shared with you one of the biggest ones.

I believe every artist needs to figure out what your cap is. Knowing how much you can handle without compromising your wellness is important. Some artists are like me. They can do several things well and happily manage them all. We have the entrepreneurial spirit, and we are managers. Others can only focus on one or two things at once and may not have an entrepreneurial spirit. There is nothing wrong with either one or any combination of the two. Today's culture glorifies entrepreneurs, but it fails to showcase how lonely and miserable that can be too.

I believe you should be yourself as an artist. If you can manage one project at a time, focus on it and make the most of it. If you can handle five projects at a time and do them well, go for it. Be yourself, and avoid falling for the pressures of doing more than you can handle. Trust me; it leads to bad places. I had my share and learned my lesson.

I would like to end my contribution to this book with one thought I think you will appreciate. It is in line with what Dr. Yanina has discussed. Honor the season in life you are in right now. Look around, and become self-aware of who you are, where you are, and what you have. Most of the time, we focus on the wrong things. We fail to exercise self-awareness. We focus on whom we wish to be based on what we see other artists do on social media. We think, *If I could only be like so and so, then I will be a more successful artist.* We focus on where we wish to be: *If only I had a bigger studio or if I was in New York, then I would be more successful.* Lastly, sometimes we focus on what we wish we had at our disposal. We wish we had more connections, more influence, more followers, more art materials, more sales—more of everything. There is nothing wrong with visualizing an ideal future and wanting more. We recommend you do that in this book. The problem arises when the focus is on your limitations.

My advice for you, my friend, as I close is this—become more self-aware and deploy more of who you already are, where you already are, and what you already have. Start there. Start with what you have now and build upon it every single day. Start your day with gratitude, prime your day with the advice found in this book, and build a better you one day at a time. Detoxify your time, relationships, and life so you too can truly live fully.

Diving Deeper

Strategy One. Identify what's important to you.

- What are the top three most important things in your life right now?

  _____

  _____

Strategy Two. Be Selective

- List activities, commitments, or events in your schedule not aligned to your goals yet take time away from what truly matters to you.

  _____

  _____

- Next to each event, write down why you're investing your time and energy in them.

  _____

  _____

As you've already learned, you're going to evaluate the investment of each situation you've listed in the previous question and make an intelligent decision. Ask yourself the following questions:

- Based on my experience so far, how is this situation contributing to my personal and professional growth?

  _____

  _____

- What are the pros and cons of being involved in this situation?

  _____

  _____

- What impact is this commitment making on my family or personal relations? Is it worth continuing with this commitment, or is it time to let it go?

  _____

  _____

- Which commitment can you potentially let go of today to open up space in your schedule and dedicate more time to what truly matters?

  _____
  _____

Starting today, before you commit to any future invitations, you'll ask yourself

- How will this invitation contribute to my personal and professional development?

  _____
  _____

- What are the pros and cons of committing?

  _____
  _____

- What impact will this invitation make on my family or personal relations if I accept it?

  _____
  _____

- Is it worth it to get involved?

  _____
  _____

Strategy Three. Define Healthy Balance Based on Your Current Life Season

- Describe the season you're currently living.

  _____
  _____

- What is your definition of a healthy balance based on your current season?

- Are you experiencing harmony or a temporary imbalance in your life?

- If you're experiencing a temporary imbalance, what needs to happen to end it?

Strategy Four. Build and Nurture a Strong Support System.

- How do you describe your inner circle?

- Do you need to detoxify your inner circle? If your answer is yes, go to question

- Starting today, begin to detoxify your relationships.

- Identify the relational vampires in your life. Write down their initials below. If you are not sure if the person is considered a relational vampire, ask yourself these questions:

- ○ Is this person there for you when you need them the most?
  _____
  _____

- ○ Does this person push you to meet your goals?
  _____
  _____

- ○ Does this person help you become the best version of yourself?
  _____
  _____

- ○ Do you feel empowered, supported, and inspired by this person?
  _____
  _____

  If you answer "no" to the questions above, will you dissolve or downgrade the relationship?
  _____
  _____

- Who can you share your doubts and fears with? Who in your life listens to you and cheers you on to be the best you can be?
  _____
  _____
  _____

- Keep them in your life.
- Invest in the relationship.
- Take a moment to text each person and thank them for being there for you.

Strategy Five. Invest in Self-Care

- Which area(s) in your physical or mental health needs your attention? How are you going to meet this need?

  _____
  _____

- Are there wounds or triggers that need professional support? What's your next step?

  _____
  _____

- Are you facing a life-changing decision? Let's break it down.

  - What are the pros and cons if you moved forward with this decision?

    _____
    _____

  - What would your life look like if you moved forward with this decision?

    _____
    _____

- What are the pros and cons if you did not move forward with his decision?
  _____
  _____

- What would your life look like if you did not move forward with this decision?
  _____
  _____

- Whom can you speak with to help you find clarity about this decision?
  _____
  _____

• How are you going to practice soul-time?

  - Write down your ideas.
    _____
    _____

  - List your joyful moments.
    _____
    _____

  - If you don't practice daily joyful moments, what adjustments need to be made to add them?
    _____
    _____

Wrapping It Up

What powerful and uplifting work you've done! You've identified what's important to you, created a plan to be more selective about the commitments in your life, defined a healthy balance for your life, reconstructed your inner circle, and identified the areas in your life that need more attention. My dear reader, have you realized how much work you've put into your inner and outer healing? I'm so proud of you for honoring your intentions and working diligently in your healing.

Before you move to the last chapter of this book, take some time to share your thoughts, takeaways, and areas you're committing to change with your accountability partner or inner circle. Do your best to remain true to your commitment to living your life to the fullest.

FINAL THOUGHTS

You can free yourself,
maximize your creativity and live fully!

"Our greatest glory is not in never falling,
but in rising every time we fall."
—Confucius

This quote speaks so much truth about our journey in this world. Life can bring opportunities, joy, satisfaction, love, success, and many wonderful experiences. It can also bring frustrations, hurdles, and disappointments. Yet, there's an indescribable feeling of satisfaction, pride, and abundant joy each time we overcome turbulent times in our lives.

In this book, you have learned strategies, tips, and ideas to help you crush self-sabotage and experience life to its fullest. In retrospect, you tuned in to your inner world and allowed yourself to dive deeper into your mind, heart, and soul. Perhaps you discovered a few things about yourself that you were unaware of, or it was more an affirmation about beliefs and ideas. You've been making healthier choices and have also come up with specific action steps to move your art career forward. Congratulations! Sergio and I are very happy for you. We hope the work you've been doing in this book has been life-changing.

If I were to tell you that from now on, you'll live a perfect life free from self-sabotage, I would be misguiding you. I would never do that! Pursuing a perfect life will rob you of amazing opportunities to grow and embrace your personal evolution. I know you're not searching for perfection. You want to live a healthier and joyful life where self-sabotage no longer has the power to shatter your creativity and success!

There will be days when you will wake up feeling like you are on top of the world. Other days, frustration and tiredness will attempt to slow you down. It's part of being human. Your inner critic will always be ready to whisper self-doubt in your ear as a response to your grit, determination, and drive. The difference this time around is you know how to stop those unwanted thoughts. You are stronger, wiser, and more determined. You're choosing possibilities over hopelessness and action over excuses. You have developed the superpower of spotting self-sabotage from a mile away and have assembled a powerful toolbox to help you overcome it again and again. You have what you need to crush self-sabotage and negative thinking!

You are not at the end of your journey toward healing. I encourage you to continue the inner work you've been intentionally doing and actively pursue your purpose and goals. As Confucius gracefully suggests, do not get stuck in the falling. We fall one way or another. When you choose to rise, it makes you more resilient, wiser, and greater. Your future will be better as you step up and take responsibility for making it happen.

This is not a goodbye. Sergio and I would love to stay in touch with you. We invite you to visit our website www.theartistnextlevel.com to learn about the Art NXT Level Academy, as well as other resources designed for artists like you, including *The Artist Next Level* podcast, Sergio's educational videos, and our blog. While you're there, sign up for our updates to stay informed about resources, art-business development events, coaching, and artist retreats.

Thank you for taking the time to read our book. We also want to thank your accountability partner or loved one for being there to support and encourage you as you worked on your inner healing. It has been an honor to walk alongside you during your journey. We look forward to hearing your story and how this book has influenced your well-being, art business, and creativity. Connect with us on all social media @artnxtlevel. Keep celebrating and sharing your wins with your accountability partner, inner circle, and loved ones.

You matter. Your art matters. Your goals and plans matter. Keep thriving and creating. The world needs the art only you can make! Above all, live your life to its fullest!

BIBLIOGRAPHY

[1] Bravata, D.M., Watts, S.A., Keefer, A.L. et al. Prevalence, Predictors, and Treatment of Impostor Syndrome: a Systematic Review. *J GEN INTERN MED* **35**, 1252–1275 (2020).

[2] Vaillant, George E.; McArthur, Charles C.; Bock, Arlie, 2022, "Grant Study of Adult Development, 1938-2000," https://doi.org/10.7910/DVN/48WRX9.

APPENDIX

MONTHLY GOAL PROGRESS TRACKING CHART

MAIN GOAL _____ MONTH _____

Action Step _____

○——————————△——————————✓

Action Step _____

○——————————△——————————✓

Action Step _____

○——————————△——————————✓

○ Start point
△ Half way done
✓ Task completed

ABOUT THE AUTHORS

Dr. A. Yanina Gomez is a psychologist, author, and speaker. She has a Doctor of Philosophy degree in Educational Psychology and has also completed the Internal Family Systems Model Training, an integrative approach to psychotherapy. She is also co-founder of The Art NXT Level Academy, an online coaching program for artists.

Dr. Yanina began her career as a psychologist working with children from pre-school to high school and helping parents raise their children in a healthier way. Her career has evolved throughout the years. Among various wellness-related projects, she teaches mindful parenting skills and how to strengthen parent-child relationships.

Throughout the years, Dr. Yanina has observed how art has the potential to affect the emotions, psychological states, and moods of people. Similarly, through coaching and numerous conversations with artists, she has witnessed how art-making can be used as a tool to ease one's tensions and release anxiety. It can also be a powerful and influential way to share the artist's voice with the world.

Dr. Yanina's understanding and insight into the psycho-emotional issues many creatives experience has allowed her to develop practical mindset and emotional wellness resources for those facing challenges in their lives and art careers. She believes people who maintain an optimal wholeness balance (mind, body, and soul) can enjoy a healthier life and make a greater impact in this world. She enjoys facilitating workshops, artist retreats, and developing resources relevant to the thriving contemporary artist. She also loves to brainstorm with artists about their career development and emotional well-being.

Dr. Yanina is the author of Moms Don't Quit! How to Influence, Empower and Stay Connected with Your Tween or Teen in a Noisy World. She has also been a guest contributor for SEEN Journal, Psychology Today's blog, ACS Magazine, and Artwork Archive blog. Finally, she is a mother of two amazing children. You're invited to follow her on social media @dryaninagomez.

Sergio Gomez is a Chicago-based visual artist. He studied at the School of the Art Institute of Chicago and received an MA degree from Governors State University and an MFA degree from Northern Illinois University. He is known for his large-scale figurative abstraction paintings and charcoal drawings exploring life cycles.

Sergio's work has been the subject of more than forty-five solo exhibitions in the United States, Romania, Italy, Mexico, and Vienna. He has participated in over 150 group exhibitions in Spain, Sweden, Mexico, Austria, Italy, South Korea, England, Cairo, Belgium, and the United States. His work is in the National Museum of Mexican Art, Brauer Museum, and other public and private collections.

Besides his studio work, Sergio Gomez is an active curator with a career of over 100 curated exhibitions since 2010.

He is the owner of 33 Contemporary Gallery, curator and director of Exhibitions at the Zhou B. Art Center, founder of Amplified Art Network, and co-founder of The Art NXT Level Academy, an online coaching program for artists.

He has curated special projects for the Chicago Park District, Chicago Garfield Park Conservatory, ArtSpot Miami International Art Fair, Museo Regionale di Scienze Naturali of Turin, National Museum of Mexican Art, and Expo Chicago Art Fair, among others.

Sergio is recognized for his online marketing and sales expertise. In 2015, he launched *The Artist NXT Level* podcast, downloaded by thousands of artists each week. With over 300 episodes, Sergio's video show provides practical advice for artists and inspires, educates, and empowers its viewers from around the world. Visit Sergio's website at www.sergiogomezonline.com or connect with him on all social media @sergiogomezart.

Online Coaching & Learning that Takes the Guessing Out of Growing Your Art Career

Boost Your Confidence, Sell More Art and Grow a Successful Art Business.

Being a successful artist today requires a confident mindset, practical marketing strategies to sell your art, business savviness, and peer support like never before.

You don't have to feel alone in your journey. Join the Art NXT Level Academy and get everything you need to stop guessing and start growing your art career once and for all.

Online Learning • Weekly Coaching • Community

We look forward to working with you!
Sergio & Dr. Yanina Gomez

Learn more:
www.theartistnextlevel.com

Bring Professional Development to Your Arts Organization, College, or University.

Lectures • Artist Talks • Workshops • Discussions

Art NXT Level offers in-depth remote and in-person learning experiences addressing the biggest challenges artists face today in their art business.

Our focus is on career strategies, marketing skills, organization, productivity, and emotional wellness.

We believe artists who adopt a wholeness approach (nurturing mind, body, and soul) can enjoy a fulfilling life and career.

Learn more:
www.theartistnextlevel.com/speaking

Hosted by Sergio Gomez, The Artist Next Level podcast features interviews with successful artists, curators, collectors, and art professionals and provides practical advice to take your art career to the next level. Join us every week to get your dose of inspiration.

Subscribe from your favorite podcast app or visit:
www.theartistnextlevel.com

www.ingramcontent.com/pod-product-compliance
Lightning Source LLC
LaVergne TN
LVHW021816060526
838201LV00058B/3413